I0559912

BREATHE

RELEASE THE PAIN AND EMBRACE YOUR PURPOSE

JAUN MALCOLM

EDITED BY

NICOLE QUEEN

VISION PUBLISHING
HOUSE

Vision Publishing House
support@vision-publishinghouse.com
www.vision-publishinghouse.com

ISBN: 978-1-955297-62-2 (print)

To the women fighting for their lives:

This book is dedicated to your strength, your perseverance, and your relentless will to move forward. May you discover light in the darkest times and experience peace in your victories.

If there's a book that you want to read, but it hasn't been written yet, then you must write it.

— TONI MORRISON

CONTENTS

PREFACE

This book is written as a testament to the unfailing love and power of Jesus Christ, who saves, heals, and delivers. His grace reaches beyond the walls of shame, brokenness, and trauma. No matter how deep the hurt or how far you may feel, you are never beyond the reach of His love.

This is a journey of transformation, where Jesus takes the shattered pieces of our lives and forms them into something beautiful. His power is for everyone the rejected, the lost, the weary, and the burdened. This book is written for the ones ready to lay down their burdens and surrender to the One who gave it all.

You are not here by accident. Jesus has called you by name. You are loved, you are cherished, and you are made whole in Him. Together, we will walk through the pages of this book toward healing, restoration, and purpose guided by the redeeming love of Jesus Christ.

Together, we will embark on a journey toward healing,
empowerment, and a purpose-driven life.

A LETTER TO MY YOUNGER SELF

Dear younger me,

I know you're hurting right now, feeling like the weight of the world is pressing down on you. The trauma, the darkness —it's all so overwhelming. There are moments when you can't see a way out, and the future seems like an unreachable dream.

But I need you to hold on. I need you to trust that this pain is not the end of your story. You are stronger than you know, and there is a light ahead that will guide you out of this darkness.

There were many nights when you cried yourself to sleep, feeling utterly alone. Yet, even in those moments, God was with you. He was holding you close, even when you couldn't feel His presence. He was your silent protector, watching over you, preparing you for the journey ahead.

As you grow, you will begin to see glimpses of that light. It will start as a small spark, barely noticeable, but it will grow. You will find strength in places you never thought to look, and slowly, you will begin to heal.

God will become your rock, your refuge, your everything. His love will surround you, filling the cracks and mending the broken pieces. You will find peace in His presence, and joy in His promises.

You will face challenges, yes, but you will also experience victories. Each step you take forward, no matter how small, is a triumph. Each moment of faith, each prayer whispered in the silence, will bring you closer to the person you are meant to be.

I am writing to you now from a place of light and strength. The shadows that once seemed so impenetrable have been chased away by the love and grace of God. He has guided you through the darkest valleys and set your feet on solid ground.

Remember that you are never alone. Even in your darkest moments, God is with you. He is your protector, your strength, and your guide. Lean on Him, trust in His plan, and know that your future is filled with hope and possibility.

You will overcome. You will rise. And you will walk in the light of God's eternal love.

With all my love and faith,
Your Future Self

INTRODUCTION

Why am I still here, having lived through what many do not survive? This question has bothered me, driving me to the brink where I believed that a world without me might be better for everyone. Who am I but a speck in this world? What can I offer anyone to help them be greater? If I didn't exist anymore, it would change nothing. Life will still continue until I am but a distant memory. Yet, here I am, a testament to a purpose that refused to let me go, to a love that sustained me when I could not sustain myself. I smile now, not because the journey has been easy, but because it has been meaningful. While death came knocking at my door, life decided not to answer. Prophetic words and fervent prayers have fortified me, spoken into the darkest moments of my life by those who saw in me what I could not.

As I reflect on the winding paths of my past, marked by tumult and the pursuit of understanding, it becomes clear that every step — every misstep — led to a greater purpose. I didn't get a lot of things right; I've failed over and over again. I've been bruised, wounded, and scarred to the point where I thought quitting would be my only answer. My waking moments felt like a thousand needles, penetrating my skin to the point that my mind would go into protection mode and take me outside of myself into a fragmented reality. It was in those moments that I became someone different, someone who wanted to not just exist but live. Yet, as I sit here today, recounting this episode from my life, I recognize that even this experience was part of my testimony, knitted together with threads of both despair and divine intervention.

The words of a well-known prophet were particularly transformative– a divine revelation that broke through my existential cocoon and propelled me into my destiny. His prophecy confirmed that within me were writings waiting to be birthed—words of encouragement and songs of hope destined to touch the lives of others. Those words brought a heaviness to my life that I couldn't shake; even though my flesh wanted me to run from the assignment, I knew I had to be obedient. This book is a fulfillment of that prophecy. Herein lies not just my story, but a call to all who feel overwhelmed by the shadows of their past to step into the light of God's promise.

God revealed to me that my struggles with confidence and self-esteem, the silent battles of my childhood where the enemy sought to steal my voice, were all part of a divine preparation. I was being prepared to use my voice not just for my healing, but to mentor and guide others, particularly young women navigating their own difficult paths. This book is my act of obedience to that divine call– a sharing of my journey to help light the way for others.

This introduction, therefore, is an invitation—a call to walk with me through the pages of this book as I share the raw, unfiltered truths of my life. It is my prayer that by sharing my story, you will find the strength to confront your own, and in doing so, discover the same profound truth that has come to define my existence: that there is purpose in the pain, and glory destined to emerge from the trials we endure.

Let us begin this journey together, with hearts open and spirits attuned to the transformative power of God's grace and divine redemption. For in the sharing of our stories, we find a common thread of resilience and a shared promise of renewal. Here's to uncovering the enduring hope that thrives even in depths of despair, and the relentless light that shines forth, undimmed by the darkest moments.

1

THE STING OF ABSENCE

In a world painted with the vibrant hues of Caribbean sunsets, with strokes of gold and crimson over the pulsing life of Jamaica, I was cradled in the strength of a West Indian woman —my mother. Have you ever wondered what it means to be truly resilient? My mother, a woman who, in many eyes, stood firm in the identity shaped by her ancestors, exemplified this resilience. Her history, like that of many others, was marked by displacement— echoed in the reggae rhythms of a well-known Jamaican singer, who sang of being stolen from Africa. Despite these historical shadows, my mother, who often proclaimed herself the black sheep of the family, emerged as a matriarch of unconquerable spirit.

From my earliest memories, my mother was a constant source of strength and joy. Her presence was a steady force in our home, her laughter a frequent echo, and her actions a testament to her unyielding love and commitment. Whether it was ensuring we had enough food, clothes, or simply her presence at the end of a school day, she was there—always protecting, always providing. Can you recall someone who made you feel safe just being there? For me, it was my mother.

One of my most vivid childhood memories was the sense of security that enveloped me as I walked the streets of our neighborhood to meet my mother after her work. In those days, the community was tight-knit, and children roamed freely, secure in the familiarity of their surroundings. One evening, as I neared her workplace, I witnessed a scene that would forever alter my perception of her. My mother was outside, fiercely confronting another person. Though initially struck by fear, my anxiety quickly transformed into admiration as I heard her voice, strong and unafraid, cutting through the tension. Have you ever seen someone you love in a new light, with their strength revealed in a moment of crisis? She was not just my mother at that moment; she was a warrior, battling not just for her dignity but for our future.

Yet, amidst this idyllic childhood, there were undercurrents of change that would soon surface. The pivotal moment came unexpectedly when my mother made a decision that would profoundly shape our lives. One day, while I slept, she left for the United States. Driven by the hope of securing a better future for us, she departed without a farewell, sparing both of us the immediate pain of a goodbye. That morning I woke up to a new reality, one where my mother's absence was a painful reminder of the sacrifices she made for our future. This experience was a sudden change that left me questioning everything.

In the wake of her departure, the home that had once been a bastion of warmth and laughter felt hollow. At the tender age of five, I could scarcely grasp the magnitude of her sacrifice; I understood only the profound sense of loss. My mother's absence left a gaping void in my heart, one that the affection of aunts, uncles, and cousins could not fill. Her smile, her laughter, her reassuring presence at dinner each evening—these were the pillars of my childhood, and without them, I found myself adrift in a sea of confusion and sorrow.

The separation from a parent at such a young age had a lasting impact on my emotional well being and development. There were times I felt abandoned, insecure, and experienced bouts of anxiety.

Despite the deep sense of abandonment, the principles my mother instilled in me remained deeply rooted. She had taught me resilience, the importance of family, and the power of unconditional love. These lessons became my guiding light as I navigated the complexities of growing up without her physical presence. Her spirit, imbued in every memory, every lesson she had imparted, continued to influence me, urging me to face life's challenges with courage and grace.

The transition was arduous. The once joy-filled family gatherings now echoed with the silence of her absence. Sundays, which had been days of communal laughter and shared meals, now carried a bittersweet tone. I remember the silence that filled our home, the empty seat at the dinner table, and the way my heart ached for her presence. Yet, in this new reality, I learned to adapt, drawing on the strength that my mother had modeled. Life without her was a challenging new normal, but it was a reality I learned to accept, fortified by the memories of her love and the enduring presence of family.

As the months turned into years, the impact of my mother's departure did not diminish. Each milestone, each achievement I made, was bittersweet, marked by the acute awareness of her absence. The sting of longing for her, the need for her guidance, protection and the desire for her approval never waned. I often found myself gazing at the stars, wondering if she too was looking up at the same sky, feeling the same aching separation. The absence of my mother left an indelible mark in my heart, a void that was felt deeply and profoundly throughout my life.

In the solitude of those nights, I began to understand the depth of her decision. It was a choice made not out of selfish desire but out of a profound love and a desperate hope for a better life for us. This realization did not erase the pain but it brought with it a new level of understanding and appreciation for the sacrifices she made.

The narrative of my childhood, woven with threads of joy and shadows of sorrow, set the stage for the person I was to become. It was a foundation built on the lessons of resilience, the power of enduring love, and the strength of family bonds. As the chapter of my life continued to unfold, it was these lessons that fortified me, nurturing my spirit and healing the wounds of separation. As the chapter of my life continued to unfold, it was these lessons that cultivated resilience, empathy, and understanding within me, shaping me into someone capable of facing the future with a sense of purpose and hope.

My grandmother moved in with us when my mother left. She was not a replacement but an added presence to help bring comfort and assurance that everything would be ok. In the protective embrace of my grandmother's arms, my world gradually expanded beyond the confines of my initial pain. My grandmother's love was a balm to my wounded heart, providing a sense of stability and continuity that was desperately needed. Her lessons weren't just about discipline; they were about the profound bonds that tie us together, about love that endures despite distance and time.

Through every ordeal and every joyous moment thereafter, the values instilled by both my mother and grandmother became my guiding principles. They taught me that life, with all its unpredictability and trials, also held infinite possibilities for growth and renewal. Each lesson, whether delivered through stern words or gentle reassurances, was a stepping stone towards becoming a person who could thrive amidst adversity.

As I matured, the image of my mother's departure, which had once symbolized loss and abandonment, transformed into a symbol of sacrifice and profound love. It became clear that her leaving was not a dismissal of her duties but rather an act of immense bravery— an attempt to lay down a better path for us, her children, even if it meant enduring the heartache of separation.

2

THE NEW NORM

In the days following my mother's departure at the age of five, I felt as if I was walking through a dense fog, each step uncertain and heavy with the weight of her absence. In this new chapter of my life, my grandmother stepped in, her presence becoming the anchor in the tumultuous sea of emotions that swirled around me. But before her stabilizing influence could take hold, I struggled with my own impulses to fill the void between my mother and me—the countless miles between us seemed like an insurmountable barrier to a child.

Haunted by the feeling of abandonment, and at times rejection, I concocted a child's plan fueled by longing and fantasy. Each day, as I sat in our yard, I let my imagination wander across continents and oceans. I envisioned a journey where I, a determined child, would trek across lands and ask strangers without fear and hesitation, if they knew where my mother, could be found. I held onto a naive hope that my journey would lead me straight to her, ending with a joyful reunion in the bustling streets of America, amidst the cacophony of honking cars and dazzling city lights. I was desperate and determined to reunite with the only one who could fill the void in my heart.

A few years later, driven by a mixture of desperation and resolve, I packed the few belongings I thought necessary for such a trek and set out on an epic journey to America. It was not as I had imagined, but my young legs carried me to the home of a nearby friend. It was a rainy, dreary evening, and as fatigue set in, I confided in my friend's family, imploring them not to inform my own of my whereabouts. In my innocence, I truly believed they would help me leave my family on this quest to find my mother. I let my guard down, feeling safe and at peace thinking it wouldn't be long before I'm back in my mother's arms. I believed my plan was foolproof, but it was not to be.

In the early hours of the morning, I awoke to the stern faces of my grandmother and uncle. The feeling of betrayal stung sharply as I realized my friend's family had not honored my request. However, nothing was more piercing than the look of quiet despair on my grandmother's face. Unlike my uncle, who expressed his frustration with stern words, my grandmother's expression conveyed a deep, silent plea, born from a mixture of relief and sorrow that I had been found safe.

Rather than the expected punishment, my grandmother sat me down and served me a warm meal. With a voice more weary than angry, she pleaded with me not to attempt such a dangerous feat again. Her words were not a warning but a heartfelt request, one that underscored her fear for my safety and her relief that nothing worse had occurred. That night, she shielded me from my uncle's anger and potential punishment, not out of leniency but from understanding and love. Her actions spoke volumes, teaching me that this home, where my mother no longer lived, was a sanctuary, not just from the outside world but from the turmoil within my own heart.

As time passed, our home dynamics evolved with the arrival of my male cousin. He came to live with us, and the responsibilities of household chores were distributed among us. However, the cultural expectations often placed a heavier burden on me because of my gender. One particular day, after completing my chores while he neglected his, my frustration boiled over. That afternoon, my grandmother was in a particularly foul mood, and our attempt to avoid her wrath led to an unexpected and somewhat humorous chase.

We dashed out of the house with my grandmother surprisingly quick on our heels. In a frantic moment of escape, he managed to leap over the fence and evade capture, while I, fumbling with the gate, was caught. The punishment I received was swift but carried out with a sense of reluctant duty rather than anger. Despite the immediate pain, the incident somehow strengthened the bond between my grandmother and me. Through her discipline, she imparted lessons of responsibility and the importance of facing consequences, yet always tempered with an undercurrent of love and understanding.

In those transformative years under my grandmother's care, I learned not just about discipline and responsibility, but about the complexities of love and the depth of family bonds. Her presence and guidance offered a semblance of the maternal love I missed, filling the void left by my mother with a different kind of affection, one that was perhaps more stern but equally profound.

Reflecting on the impact of those years, I understood that my grandmother's lessons were preparing me for life's broader challenges. They taught me resilience, the value of emotional fortitude, and the importance of understanding others' actions, even when they initially seem harsh or unfair.

3
SECRETS

Children are supposed to grow up in environments where the loudest noises are laughter and playful shouts. As a child, the world outside seemed vast and full of opportunities for joy and exploration. Across from our two-story home was a park—a magnet for the neighborhood kids and a place where I sought refuge and companionship. We played seemingly innocent games like tag and throwing rocks, while not fully understanding that these were subtle rehearsals for understanding strength and resilience. The same rocks that we hurled at each other were also used to knock almonds from the trees. We'd eagerly split open the hard shells to extract the nuts, a symbolic act that paralleled the way life seemed to crack us open to reveal our inner strengths or frailties. This metaphor became painfully literal in the way my peers used personal attacks as their stones.

This same playground became a battleground where words turned into weapons. They knew about my mother's departure to America and my father's absence, facts that they twisted into sharp-tipped darts aimed directly at my vulnerabilities. The taunts about my absent mother and absent father cut deeper than the physical scrapes of play. My peers did not hold back in reminding me that I was alone, unloved by the very people who should have cared for me the most. "Nobody wants you," they'd shout, or "You're so ugly, that's why your mom left." At first, I tried to shield myself with indifference, but resilience in the face of such relentless cruelty can only stretch so far. Each word struck with the precision of a well-aimed rock, leaving emotional bruises deep inside my heart.

One day, the taunts became unbearable. A boy, with a sneer and a jeer about my mother not loving me, followed me relentlessly. His words were like daggers, each one puncturing the facade of toughness I had tried so hard to maintain. "Your mom didn't love you enough to stay," he jeered, with a chorus of laughter from others trailing behind him. That laughter, so light for them, was a weight on my chest, pressing until the air thinned and my vision tunneled into a pinpoint of red. My reaction was visceral; anger replaced the hurt, a raging fire where tears might have been.I turned on him in fury, my small fists flailing, connecting with his body, driven by a strong need for him to just stop. I hated him at that moment; I hated him for exposing my fears. My friends had to pull me away, but even as they did, I felt a terrifying strength within me fueled by rage and pain.

After this explosion of emotion, doubts about my mother's love began to infect my thoughts. She had moved on, I believed, to a better life without me—one where she was happier without the burden of a child. Though she still called and sent gifts, the physical void she left was vast and filled with shadows. Each subsequent phone call or package from her, meant to bridge our distance, instead emphasized the miles and silence between us. The gifts felt like apologies, and the calls felt like reminders of a bond strained, yet possibly broken. Therefore, I built a wall around my heart, distancing myself from her to protect myself from further disappointment and hurt.

As I grappled with these feelings, a dark cloud encroached on my life. I was forced to remember that at the age of five, this rage and void began. I was introduced to betrayal at a very young age. During my time of learning a new norm of not having my mother around, darkness swept into my life. This darkness walked in and stole everything that I thought was good. An older relative made advances on me, shattering my once firm foundation. He broke in me what I knew to be good. I told no one, out of fear. This violation, confusing and deeply scarring, marked the beginning of a series of betrayals that would shape my early adolescence. This dark secret, now lodged within me, became a source of shame and further isolation. I was too young to fully understand the implications, but I knew enough to feel dirty, used, and tarnished by an act meant to exploit rather than protect. I was alone—all alone in my pain. I began to believe the words of the neighborhood kids: "you're nothing and worth nothing." Could they be right? The mind is a powerful thing, and in desperation, it quickly built a wall of protection to shut myself away from the sting of betrayal. I entered a dark pit that day, trying to hide the stain of filth that had become a part of my identity.

This betrayal was not an isolated incident. This violation of trust was the first of several by different predators. Watching Animal Planet, I always admired lions. They were ferocious creatures that no one dared go against. Known as predators, they knew how to blend into any environment and wait to pounce on their prey, destroying it. This is how I viewed my predators who lay in wait in the shadows, stalking me, waiting for the perfect moment to pounce and destroy everything that was me. Each encounter taught me that vulnerability could be dangerous. Over time, I encountered others who saw my vulnerability as something to exploit. My brokenness was an invitation to be violated. The devil only needs an inch to wreak chaos on the lives of people. Knowing now what I didn't then, he wanted to destroy my identity before I came into the realization that I was marked by a more powerful source; God. The enemy of my soul tried to kill me before I could destroy him and his kingdom.

A memory of a friend, a trusted young adult known to everyone in the community, was also another predator during an innocent game of hide-and-seek. His attempt to molest me under the guise of play was thwarted only by my own panic and sudden aggression, leaving me shaken and even more distrustful of those around me. Confusion settled in, not able to wrap my mind around the sudden invasion that kept finding me. "Was it something I said or did?" Those thoughts began to play on repeat in my mind, causing me to become suspicious of all who dared to come close to me. I told no one. I thought no one would believe me because this predator was a friend, someone we all knew. It was then that people became looming shadows of pure evil in my eyes. They hovered over me in the pit of despair, lashing out, trying to reach me– only to hurt me. Closeness became a suffocating grave where I could hardly breathe. The restriction I felt helped me to grow silent. Only I could hear the screams from within.

You see, the pit for me was a place of despair. It was a place of silent screams where no one could hear them. In the beginning, it was dark, gloomy, and smelled of death. It was a place where you wished for death to take away the pain because it felt like no one cared for you.you're alone, abandoned and rejected. Every trauma that came, any chance to survive was robbed. It only made me sink deeper and deeper into despair. The persons that violated me mishandled my soul and rejected me. My emotional well being was destroyed to the point that I couldn't even see myself, and I didn't want to because I hated what I saw. I didn't want to be here.

The enemy tried to take away the one thing that kept me fighting: my voice. You become your own greatest enemy when you can't see any light. No light, no hope. It's like nobody can see you, and you aren't worth saving. It's as if you become so unrecognizable to yourself that even people who love you can't help you because they don't know how.

These experiences compounded the isolation I felt, turning my early life into a series of defensive maneuvers and retreats. I learned to erect barriers, to anticipate pain or betrayal from any quarter, and to trust no one completely. The word "love" became a trigger, a precursor to pain, something professed by those who would later show their true intentions in the worst ways possible. Love was a blanket of lies; it was a cheat code to gain access to the good in you to be mishandled, only to then turn around and destroy you.

As the years passed, the burden of these secrets and the weight of my unresolved anger and sadness grew heavier. I withdrew further, pushing away opportunities for closeness or affection because they felt fraught with potential danger. My world contracted to a few safe corners where the shadows of past traumas lured me in.

Excitement filled me when my family needed a larger place to live. We hoped for a fresh start, but the past's shadows loomed large. which brought new faces and the promise of new beginnings. But even there, challenges followed. Darkness relocated with us.

An incident with a neighbor, who grew close to me over the months — became enraged when I refused her romantic advances and threatened me with scalding water and unleashed her dog on me in a fit of rage—reinforced my wariness of forming close relationships. This incident further underscored a recurring theme in my life: those who professed to care for me often harbored the deepest capacity to inflict pain. The physical pain of the boiling water that seared my skin was a reminder of the emotional scars I carried; it was a painful reminder that trust was a luxury I might never afford.

Through these trials, I learned to view love and affection with suspicion, associating these words with the pain and betrayal that seemed inevitably to follow. The word 'love' became tainted, a token of deceit that masked ulterior motives. 'Love' was suffocating. I also learned to bury my pain, to lock away the hurt and pretend it didn't exist. Survival meant adapting, excusing the inexcusable, and often blaming myself. "It's my fault," became a mantra, a way to make sense of the senseless. This self-blame was a defense mechanism, a shield against the realization that those who were supposed to love and protect me often brought the most harm.

4
THE CHALLENGE OF TRANSITION

As time moved on and I continued to grow, I learned that nobody prepares you for the pain of loss. No one warns you how deeply grief can sting. My world was turned upside down by the sudden illness of my beloved grandmother. She, who was always a beacon of joy and vitality, began to fade before my very eyes. It was a decline so stark, so rapid, that it seemed an intruder had invaded her body, sapping her strength day by day.

Her transformation was alarming. The grandmother I knew—always singing, always smiling—became increasingly lethargic, her once vibrant spirit dimmed by an unseen ailment. Watching her in the hospital then at home became places I associated with despair. I seldom visited the hospital, not just out of fear but because seeing her so altered pained me deeply. Once she was home, seeing her shrink before me communicated to my childlike mind that hope was a lie.

No one spoke explicitly about her illness, about the cancer that was ravaging her colon. I only discovered its name and its lethal nature much later in life. But even as a child, witnessing her physical deterioration—her body becoming frail, her skin clinging to her bones— I sensed the inevitability of what was to come. She was no longer the woman who had raised me with songs and stories; she was a shadow, bedridden and fragile, a stark reminder of mortality's cruel reach. Death came knocking at her door, but I kept it shut, refusing its entry into our home.

Amidst this personal turmoil, life's relentless pace pulled me in another direction—the prospect of traveling to the United States for the first time. I was good at running. I felt great freedom while racing my peers and winning. I was good at something that no one could take from me. At home, I would race my aunt, always believing I would win, but she never let me. I admired her long strides and how fast she was. The opportunity came where I could represent my school in Miami at a track meet. My 10-year-old self was excited. I had never traveled outside of Jamaica before and was desperate for the experience. My family quickly got my traveling documents together, and all I needed now was a day and time to fly. However, another opportunity arose for me to visit my mother in New York for the weekend. The excitement of such an adventure was overshadowed by my grandmother's condition. She didn't seem to be getting better. The thought of leaving her, even for a weekend, filled me with dread. Despite the years that had passed since I last saw my mother, the reconnection was fraught with anxiety. Would she recognize me? Would the bond we once shared still exist?

Reluctantly, I went to where my grandmother laid, to bid her farewell, promising to return soon. The tears in her eyes mirrored my own, a silent exchange of sorrow and unspoken fears. It was a heart-wrenching goodbye.

The journey to the airport was a blur of familiar landscapes, each sight a stab of guilt as I moved further from my ailing grandmother. The tears I fought back were a mix of excitement and profound sadness, a cocktail of emotions that left me feeling hollow inside. I took flight alone, under the watchful eyes of the flight attendants. The journey wasn't long but the distance was wide.

Arriving in New York was a surreal experience. The reunion with my mother was emotional and healing, a brief respite from the ache of impending loss. Her embrace was warm and genuine, a momentary shelter from the storm of emotions that had accompanied me across the ocean. Looking into her warm brown eyes, I saw familiarity looking back at me. Her round face, beautiful wide smile, and perfect peace gave me a sense of home. She was the same mother I remembered, though years had separated us; she remained unchanged. Yet, even in her arms, I could not shake the dread that clung to my spirit.

Hours after my arrival in New York, my mother received the dreaded call—my grandmother had passed away. The news shattered any semblance of joy or relief I had felt. The guilt of having left her side was overwhelming, compounded by the helplessness of being so far from home at such a crucial time. I froze. I showed no emotions; I couldn't. Death snuck in while I was gone and stole my heart away. I felt betrayed by my own decision to leave, tormented by the irrational but piercing thought that my absence had somehow contributed to her demise. As I sat in my bedroom, looking around at what was unfamiliar to me—new clothes, new home, new everything—I realized this would be my new residence. The guilt was suffocating, compounded by the sudden permanence of my stay in the United States. What was meant to be a short visit morphed into an indefinite relocation, and with it, the loss of everything familiar. I began to fight to breathe. Overwhelmed by the sudden changes, I did the only thing I knew to do in order to cope—I shut down. I barely spoke.

Navigating this new reality was challenging. Starting school in New York presented new challenges. The cultural differences were jarring, from the casual attire in schools to the linguistic nuances that set me apart from my peers.The days that followed were a blur of grief and adjustment. I struggled to fit into a system that felt alien. My classmates' curiosity about my speech and my teachers' doubts about my academic abilities added layers of frustration to my already heavy heart. My accent and expressions, remnants of my

Jamaican upbringing, were sometimes points of ridicule. This helped to paint my school days with shades of isolation and frustration.

In this new world, I grappled with my identity and the loss of the woman who had been a cornerstone of my life. The cultural differences between Jamaica and the United States were stark, and each day was a battle to find my footing. The pain of my grandmother's death, the disorientation of immersion in a new culture, and the challenges of navigating the educational system were overwhelming.

One day, unable to bear the weight of my emotions, I broke down completely. The floodgates opened, and I cried for everything—the grandmother I'd lost, the family I'd left behind, and the childhood that had been taken from me too soon. It was a moment of utter despair, a culmination of all the trials I had faced.

Despite these hurdles, a ray of hope shone through in the form of my fifth-grade teacher. Her kindness and understanding provided a much-needed sanctuary from the storms that raged within me. She was a pillar of support, helping me navigate both my grief and the academic challenges I faced. Her classroom became a place of solace, where I could begin to piece together my fragmented sense of self.

In the solitude of my new life, One random day, I found myself outside gazing at the sky, shouting at a God I had never believed in—a God my grandmother had adored. In these moments, I unleashed all my anger and sorrow, blaming Him for not saving her, declaring my refusal to accept or understand such divine choices. It was a release of pain, a cathartic denial of faith that somehow brought a brief respite from my anguish.

5
THE JOKE OF THE UNIVERSE

Time waits for no one, and so I rolled with it. As I entered my teenage years, slumber parties became a desire of mine.It would show I belonged and was accepted into a group. They seemed a rite of passage, a way to forge friendships in the landscape of adolescence, yet they introduced new conflicts and challenges that I was scarcely prepared for. My mother, a nurse often working night shifts, instilled strict rules about safety and trust, emphasizing the dangers of our surroundings compared to the communal warmth of Jamaica. Her warnings were clear: "Do not open the door to anyone claiming I sent them." These instructions, meant to protect, also sowed seeds of fear and isolation in me, intensifying my sense of being an outsider in a sprawling, unfamiliar city.

During her absences, I stayed with a family she knew that were seemingly good. They attended church faithfully and witnessed to me the goodness of God. Despite their kindness, my already fragile trust in divinity and community had been shattered by previous betrayals. I harbored a deep skepticism of their faith and intentions, a protective shield against further disappointment. Their daughter, a seemingly innocuous figure, became another source of discomfort.

Her actions at these sleepovers, subtle yet invasive, reminded me painfully of my past vulnerabilities. One night, as I tried to sleep, I felt her hand uncomfortably close, reigniting old fears and confusion. After telling her "no" repeatedly and rejecting any form of advances, she explicitly crossed my boundaries. It was then I realized with chilling clarity that she viewed me not as a friend but as an object for her desires.

The situation escalated until I couldn't bear to stay in that house any longer. I confided in my mother a need to no longer return, in which she respected my wishes and agreed not to send me there again. I didn't tell her what happened to me out of fear of what may happen. These people were her friends, and I wanted to stay away from anything that may break the normalcy of what we tried to portray– a good family.

With more time alone, I turned to my old hobbies from Jamaica —drawing and writing. I found my voice in the arts. These activities became my sanctuary, allowing me to channel my emotions and thoughts into art and poetry. As I sketched and wrote, I began to process my experiences, transforming my pain into creative expressions that others admired. This recognition was a balm to my scarred self-esteem, slowly nurturing a sense of worth that had been eroded by my experiences.

However, my respite was short-lived. Another family friend and her son entered my life, initially offering a semblance of normalcy and safety. But this too was compromised when her interest in me took an unsettling turn. Her assumptions about my sexuality, based on superficial observations, were both invasive and unwelcome. My insecurities and wanting to be invisible called for me to dress the part. Loose jeans and shirts hid me away from lurking eyes and predators' advances– or so I thought. I trusted her. She was kind and understanding, like a big sister I never had. Things shifted after a while. Her advances, when I stayed over, confirmed my worst fears— that my past was not behind me but an ongoing cycle I couldn't escape. She crossed a line that she couldn't come back from. Her actions left me questioning my worth, reinforcing a deep-seated belief that I somehow deserved this treatment. Creation was against me, and I was the joke of the universe. With every attack, the air around me became thicker and heavier to breathe in.

These incidents pushed me further into isolation. I withdrew from those around me, building walls so high that even my mother couldn't see the pain I was hiding. I internalized the belief that I was fundamentally flawed, unworthy of genuine affection or respect. This mindset led me into darker places, where self-hatred and despair overshadowed the brief moments of joy I found in art and friendship.

In school, I maintained a facade of compliance and achievement, which masked the turmoil within. My teachers saw a quiet, diligent student, unaware of the internal battles that raged silently. My mother, proud of my academic success, remained oblivious to my emotional struggles, interpreting my quiet nature as a sign of stability rather than a cry for help.

The culmination of these experiences came one night at my best friend's house, where the familiar pattern of unwanted advances reoccurred. She trespassed onto my body. I was worn down by the constant battles to assert my boundaries and as the situation escalated, a renewed sense of self-preservation surged within me. I rejected the advances, reclaiming a shred of dignity and control by leaving the situation physically, walking home in the early morning hours, ending a friendship that was cultivated for years before. It came to an abrupt end and left me emotionally scarred.

6

IDENTITY CRISIS

In everyday life, there are chapters that mark significant transformations—mine was no exception. As a child, I was the quiet one in class, known for my diligence and obedience. Teachers filled my report cards with praises, foreseeing a bright academic future. But beneath this veneer of a model student, storms of confusion and pain were brewing, destined to alter my path dramatically.

As adolescence beckoned, the impact of early traumas began to manifest in ways I hadn't anticipated. The classroom, once a sanctuary of learning and achievement, turned into a stage for my rebellion. I transformed from the quiet child into someone almost unrecognizable, driven by a tumultuous inner world. I started to act out, seeking attention not for accolades but for antics, turning into the class clown to mask the turmoil within.

This behavioral shift was not just about seeking attention; it was a deeper cry for help. The attacks I had endured, the trust I had placed in those who betrayed me—these experiences started to erode my sense of self. Questions about my identity, particularly my sexuality, began to surface with painful insistence. The more I was hurt by those I trusted, the more I questioned whether there was something inherent in me that invited such betrayals. I started gravitating towards the wrong crowd—the misfits, rebels, and those who would embrace the misfit in me.

Amidst this identity crisis, I faced an internal conflict intensified by societal stigmas and personal shame. Accepting an identity that felt imposed upon me by my experiences, I grappled with deep-seated confusion and self-loathing. I rebelled against everything I had known, including my own self-image, which I could no longer bear to embrace. This rebellion was not just external; it was a profound upheaval of everything I thought I knew about myself.

In a desperate attempt to cope, I distanced myself from the academic excellence I once held dear. My grades began to slip, my interactions with teachers grew contentious, and I frequently found myself in detention or in front of the principal's office. This academic decline was a visible marker of the chaos within, reflecting my struggle to find a footing in a world that seemed to constantly shift under my feet. I felt like a wild lion trying to protect itself and its environment from intruders. I wanted everyone to stay away but also to see me. A rage began to build inside me from the frustration of the trauma cycles and from being misunderstood. I questioned why no one dug deeper to find the root of my problems.

My home life, too, felt the impact of my internal strife. I wanted desperately for my mother to see the changes in me—to recognize them as signs of deeper issues and to offer help. Yet, communication between us had frayed, tangled in misunderstandings and mutual hurt. Where I once saw a potential ally in her, I now felt only the widening chasm of disconnect.

The estrangement from my mother and my educational struggles pushed me further into risky behaviors. Alcohol became a refuge, providing temporary relief from the relentless self-doubt and identity questions. I knew the dangers, the slippery slope I was on, but the brief moments of oblivion it offered were too enticing to resist.

My exploration of identity led me to online spaces and new social circles, where I encountered individuals who seemed to accept and understand the facets of me that I was only beginning to acknowledge. These friendships, formed in chat rooms and solidified in city parks and movie theaters, were a double-edged sword. They offered belonging but also introduced me to even riskier behaviors. My ventures into these relationships were tentative at first, driven by a desire to fit in somewhere, anywhere.

As I delved deeper into these new social settings, I began to experiment more boldly with my identity, adopting labels that seemed to fit the expectations of those around me rather than my own understanding of myself. This experimentation extended to my sexuality, where I allowed others to define my experiences, often at the cost of my own comfort and consent.

In high school, marijuana and clubbing added layers to my rebellion, providing both an escape from and a reinforcement of the chaos within. Each puff of smoke, each night spent dancing away my troubles, seemed to further detach me from the person I had once been. Yet, with each act of defiance, I sank deeper into a morass of confusion and self-doubt.

The culmination of these experiences was a paradoxical blend of liberation and entrapment. On the one hand, I felt free from the constraints of my previous identity, emboldened to explore who I might truly be. On the other, I was caught in a web of behaviors and influences that pulled me further from any real understanding of myself.

Reflecting on this turbulent chapter of my life, I see it as a crucial period of growth, albeit painful and fraught with mistakes. It was a time when the foundations of my identity were both challenged and reshaped, leading me through darkness towards a gradual, hard-won enlightenment.

7
ACTS OF REBELLION

Adolescence, often painted as a time of discovery and growth, morphed into a nightmarish landscape for me. The previous chapters of life left scars too deep, breeding a turmoil that I could neither escape nor fully understand. My actions, once grounded in the pursuit of academic excellence and familial approval, shifted dramatically. I began to cut myself, a physical manifestation of the internal pain that seemed to suffocate my every waking moment.

The descent began subtly, with small acts of rebellion against my own body and soul. Each cut on my wrist was a desperate attempt to feel something—anything—other than the emotional numbness that had enveloped me. The sight of blood served as a stark, visceral reminder that I was still alive, still breathing, despite feeling so utterly dead inside.

This period was marked not just by physical self-harm but by a profound questioning of my very existence. "Why am I alive?" "What is my purpose?" These questions haunted me, echoing through my mind with every heartbeat. The answers seemed just as painful as the questions: I felt like a mistake, an anomaly in the fabric of life.

To drown out these thoughts, I turned to alcohol and marijuana. They were temporary salves, substances that could dull the sharp edges of my reality. Under their influence, I could float away from the burden of consciousness, from the relentless self-loathing and identity confusion that had become my constant companions.

However, the escape they offered was fleeting. Sobriety brought back all the pain and confusion, hitting harder each time. The cycle of self-medication grew into a lifestyle—drinking, smoking, anything to keep the crushing reality at bay. But the more I numbed myself, the more I lost touch with the person I once aspired to be.

My academic performance, once a source of pride, faltered badly. I was failing, not just in school, but in every aspect of life that mattered. My relationships with family—particularly with my mother—were strained to the breaking point. I yearned for her to see my pain, to recognize the silent cries for help that I masked with a facade of toughness. Yet, every attempt to reach out seemed to widen the chasm between us.

In this state of desperation, I ventured further into the world of sexual exploration. It was a realm that promised acceptance and attention, albeit of a kind that often left me feeling more used than valued. My interactions with both men and women became increasingly transactional, a way to feel wanted, even if only for a moment. Perversion was at its height, and had its way with me. The best way to describe the torment in my mind can be found in Romans 7:15-20.

"I do not understand what I do. For what I want to do I do not do, but what I hate I do. And if I do what I do not want to do, I agree that the law is good. As it is, it is no longer I myself who do it, but it is sin living in me. For I know that good itself does not dwell in me, that is, in my sinful nature. For I have the desire to do what is good, but I cannot carry it out. For I do not do the good I want to do, but the evil I do not want to do—this I keep on doing. Now if I do what I do not want to do, it is no longer I who do it, but it is sin living in me that does it."

— ROMANS 7:15-20

The confusion about my sexual identity, exacerbated by my experiences and the societal stigmas attached to them, deepened. I adopted labels— lesbian, bisexual, gay— not out of a true under-standing of myself, but as costumes to wear in various contexts, hoping one would eventually fit and define me.

Yet, each label felt like another layer of disguise, distancing me further from understanding who I really was. My sexual encounters, whether with men or women, were acts of performance, where I mimicked intimacy without ever truly feeling it. Pornography became both a teacher and a tormentor, shaping my behaviors but never satisfying the deep longing for genuine connection.

The spiral continued, each day a blend of concealment and display, each night a plunge into behaviors that promised oblivion but delivered only deeper despair. The enemy, as I came to see my own destructive impulses, was not just external but within, a voice constantly whispering that I was unworthy of love, life, or happiness.

I found stability in a job I enjoyed as a young adult. I kept to myself, and no one bothered me. I was one of the few females working in the office. A few men befriended me; I found them funny, non-threatening, and even better, they were married. Our friendship grew over time, even extending to meeting and spending time with their loved ones. They became like brothers to me. An opportunity arose to go to Atlantic City, and I jumped on it. We drank, smoked, laughed, and had a good time. I don't recall leaving the casino to go to my hotel room, but I do remember waking up to my "brother" on top of me, violating what dignity I had left. I think I actually stopped breathing in those moments. I went completely numb. When he was finished, he acted as if nothing had happened, seemingly proud of himself. I didn't speak the entire way home, nor did I ever return to my job.

As I navigated my course, the few glimmers of concern from friends and fleeting moments of self-awareness were not enough to pull me from the edge. Instead, they were brief pauses in the relentless march toward self-annihilation. It was a march that seemed destined to end in tragedy, with each step driven by a profound loss of hope and a deepening belief that perhaps the world would indeed be better off without me.

8

BREAKING BOUNDARIES

Navigating through my young adult years, I was entrenched in a lifestyle that was both a shield and a shackle. Having graduated from high school, started college and secured a job, I felt an illusory sense of control over my life. Yet, beneath this façade, I was still grappling with the shadows cast by my past. I continued to assert my identity as gay, driven by a misguided mission to influence others as I had been, perpetuating a cycle of pain under the guise of empowerment.

At my new job, I encountered a spectrum of relationships that only served to complicate my life further. During this period, I also forged a friendship with a male colleague who mirrored my own hedonistic tendencies. He was charismatic and enjoyable to be around, often inviting me over for drinks. Although there was an unspoken sexual tension, it wasn't until one impulsive night that we crossed that boundary. This developed into an arrangement where sexual encounters could be initiated without preamble, a setup that persisted without complication until he began dating another coworker. His new relationship introduced tensions that I had no desire to exacerbate, so I ended our arrangement to avoid drama.

However, one reckless night at a club, filled with a mix of vodka, Patron, rum, and beer, led to a loss of control I hadn't anticipated. The evening ended at his house, where, in my inebriated state, I became vulnerable in a way I had vowed never to allow again. I awoke on his couch to find him exploiting that vulnerability, shattering the remnants of trust between us. This act of betrayal dredged up past traumas, reinforcing my feelings of powerlessness and reigniting my deepest fears of abandonment and misuse.

Shaken by the incident, I sought escape in even more destructive ways. My coping mechanisms evolved from alcohol and marijuana to more potent substances. In a moment of profound despair, I turned to ecstasy, hoping to find some semblance of peace or oblivion. The experience under the drug's influence was surreal, providing a temporary respite from my internal turmoil, but it was a fleeting escape that could not erase the deep scars left by continuous betrayal.

As the darkness deepened, I withdrew further, building walls around my heart that were impenetrable. The cycle of using and being used became a norm, and my life a series of transactions devoid of genuine connection. Each new violation left me more isolated, fueling a descent into a solitude that was as comforting as it was suffocating.

In this abyss, the moments of light—the fleeting joys and brief encounters with happiness—were overshadowed by an ever-present darkness. The weight of my experiences bore down on me, each day a battle against the encroaching despair. The struggle to find meaning in the chaos, to discern a reason to continue amidst such relentless pain, became the central narrative of my life.

9
JESUS, SAVE ME!

I t's astounding how, in moments of deep unraveling, your world begins to spin out of control—and mine was spinning wildly. I saw no means to halt its tumultuous rotation, nor did I harbor the desire to try. Reflecting on that mindset, I recall the haze of daily intoxication, branding myself as a functional alcoholic and druggie with a dismissive laugh, as if it were perfectly normal. I never hesitated in my actions, driven by a belief that true living required pushing boundaries and experimenting with everything. After all, how else could one truly discover what they liked?

I had always been laid back, the kind of person others gravitated towards for my easygoing nature. I avoided conflicts and maintained a cool demeanor, yet I began to notice a shift within myself. Irritation crept into my once calm existence; suddenly, the person known for her chill attitude was irritated by everything. The nightlife lost its appeal; I preferred the solitude of my apartment to the crowded dance floors I once frequented.

During this period, I decided to move out of my mother's house in my early 20s. I felt like an adult and didn't want my mother to intervene in my affairs. I was living with a friend who became my girlfriend. She moved in with me for a considerable time. Our shared space became a source of discomfort; I found myself recoiling from her touch and snapping at her words. It was clear to both of us that something profound was amiss, yet I remained indifferent to her concern. I wanted her to leave, but I couldn't voice it. I longed for change but was mute on how or what precipitated the feeling of emptiness that was swallowing me whole. This growing void inside was a chasm I tried to fill with alcohol, but the more I drank, the deeper it grew. The only emotion I could muster towards myself was disdain.

I hated myself; every aspect of my being was a source of disdain. The mere contemplation of my actions filled me with nausea, leaving me embarrassed, ashamed, rejected, and utterly isolated. Childhood traumas resurfaced, haunting my thoughts, and driving me to seek oblivion in alcohol just to silence my mind. Suddenly, everything became a trigger. Rainfall seemed a personal affront, worsening what was already a dreadful day. A gusty wind felt like a physical attack as if the very elements were conspiring against me. This constant state of turmoil left me seething with anger towards everything and everyone around me.

Thus, the woman, living with me, began inviting people over to the apartment, which invariably irked me. I would insist, "They need to leave. I don't want them here." When she protested that they were her friends, my response was dismissive—I didn't care; they had to go. Since it was my apartment, I had the final authority on such matters.

However, I reached a near-breaking point during the preparation for my birthday celebration. I had invited a few close friends over to relax and enjoy ourselves at my apartment. A good friend was helping me set up; we were sharing a smoke, eagerly anticipating the evening ahead. As we lounged in my bedroom, my girlfriend surreptitiously took my car keys from their usual spot on the kitchen table and left without a word. I was oblivious to her departure until a persistent, unknown number began calling my phone. Initially, I ignored the calls, distracted by the festivities, but the relentless ringing eventually drew my attention.

When I finally decided to answer, the caller had hung up. Moments later, my girlfriend returned, laughing as she entered—her laughter immediately grated on me. She then explained, with an unsettling casualness, that she had taken my car without permission to run to the store and had been involved in an accident. My heart sank as she described how another vehicle had T-boned mine, effectively totaling it by smashing into the side. The visual of my car bent into a 'V' shape was too much to bear. To make matters worse, she admitted she let the other driver go because she wasn't legally supposed to be behind the wheel. Overwhelmed by anger and betrayal, I exploded in a furious tirade, my emotions boiling over with shouts and curses; I was so enraged, I felt like I could have done something drastic.

The rage that erupted from me was unprecedented, fueled by the immediate concern: "How will I commute to work in Long Island from Queens without a car?" The sheer inconvenience was maddening, not to mention that she had never been given permission to take my car. Why would she do that? And then to let the other driver go— it was unfathomable. I felt utterly betrayed, and there was no forgiving her this time. This girlfriend wasn't just any friend; she was someone I had known since middle school. Our long history had built a trust that was now shattered by her actions.

The sense of betrayal deepened during another incident when a friend from Connecticut visited, and we decided to attend a cookout. The drive there was uneventful, but on the return journey, something my girlfriend did or said—though I can't recall exactly what— infuriated me. We had been cautious not to drink much, knowing we had a long drive home. Yet, as we drove on the highway, her actions provoked me so intensely that in a moment of frustration, I aggressively jerked the steering wheel to switch lanes. This abrupt maneuver caused our car to collide with another vehicle on the road.

As I struggled to regain control, the car began to spin wildly on the highway. I reassured myself, convinced by past experiences that I could realign the car. As I managed to steer it back into the right lane, another vehicle, attempting to swerve out of the way, collided with us. Our car tipped onto two wheels, teetered momentarily, then crashed back down, beginning a terrifying roll. In that instant, a grim realization struck me: "I'm dead." The car continued to tumble end over end, a relentless cascade of flips across the asphalt. Sparks flew in all directions, the sound of shattering glass filled the air, and the screech of metal dragging on the road echoed ominously. There was no time for screams or thoughts; we were utterly consumed by the immediacy of the catastrophe.

Amid the chaos and spiraling destruction, much like my own life, a profound fear gripped me. "Oh my God, this will devastate my mother if I die here," I thought. In that critical moment, instinctively, I turned to prayer. I reached out to Jesus, despite our long silence: "Jesus, we haven't spoken in a while, but please, spare my life. My mother can't bear losing me, not like this." This plea was a desperate bid from someone staring down death.

There seemed to be no escape. The imminent dangers were clear —either a ditch, a wall, a tree, or another vehicle was about to end everything. Amid the shower of sparks and the roar of destruction, I prayed aloud, "Jesus, save me, if you do, I'll go to church and serve you." The words came instinctively, a cry to the heavens, not knowing from where within me they arose. As soon as my prayer ended, the car miraculously came to a halt as if guided by divine intervention. Those of faith would argue it was not by chance but by God's hand that death was averted. As the car ceased its violent tumbling, my friends quickly escaped the wreckage. I remained, suspended upside down, my seatbelt the only thing between me and further harm, my hand bracing against the car's roof.

As the disorientation set in and blood rushed to my head, voices outside called to me, urging me to get out. But shock had rooted me in place. Eventually, they returned, unfastened my seatbelt, and guided me toward what they saw as the safest exit. The only way out was through the trunk, the car doors hopelessly crushed. As I crawled through the wreckage, bracing for the agony I was sure would come, I feared the worst. Emerging from the trunk, bracing for pain, I found none. I stood, inspected my hands, my body—miraculously, there was no blood, no sign of injury.

When I finally turned to see my friends, they were unharmed. There was no blood, no broken bones; nobody was limping. Glancing back at my car, I was struck by a profound realization—it was only by divine intervention that we survived. The vehicle was twisted and mangled beyond recognition, like foil crumpled into a tight ball by a giant hand. It was utterly destroyed, and yet, miraculously, we all walked away without a scratch. Onlookers rushed towards us, bewildered but relieved to find us all okay, checking us for injuries they expected but found absent.

Then, as the ambulance arrived, the paramedics sprang into action, immediately assessing everyone's condition. They insisted on me, the driver, wearing a neck brace, explaining, "There could be internal damage; you might be bleeding inside, and we can't take any chances." Despite our protests, they were adamant: we had to go to the hospital. Reluctantly, we complied, and at the hospital, after thorough checks, they found us all remarkably, inexplicably fine.

Standing in the hospital, a promise I had made to myself echoed in my mind—I had to go to church. I contacted the only person I knew who could guide me in this commitment, my aunt. She had been inviting me to church for years, often telling me, "Jesus saves. He loves you. You need to change your life, turn it around; you're a sinner." I had dismissed her and told her to leave me alone. But now, humbled and grateful, I reached out to her, asking, "Hey, I'm coming to church. What time is the service, and what do I wear?" Thus, on Easter Sunday, 2008, I found myself entering a church, ready to honor a vow made in a moment of desperation.

While entering the church that day, I was acutely aware of not fitting in. Surrounded by congregants who seemed to hold themselves above others, I felt alienated. To me, churchgoers appeared sanctimonious, convinced of their own perfection. Their judgment and lack of empathy had always struck me as hypocritical, more about condemnation than support. My past experiences were that their behaviors, their quickness to criticize rather than understand someone's background or struggles, had left a sour taste.

So there I was, stepping into what felt like a den of lions. I felt like the prey walking to a painful death. Determined to remain unnoticed, I took a seat near the back, keeping to myself while secretly counting the minutes until I could leave. The longer I sat amongst the congregants, the more exposed I felt. Hidden in my car were the familiar comforts of blunts and small bottles of vodka, ready for me when I could escape this place.I felt like I was in a pit of darkness, ready to be swallowed up in sin. Yet, I was there to fulfill a promise, thinking to myself, "I'm here; He can't claim I never showed up," referring to God.

As I sat waiting for the service to end, the pastor took to the pulpit on that crowded Easter Sunday of 2008. He delivered a sermon that unnervingly seemed to narrate my life. Every word resonated as though it was tailored for me. I grew incensed, suspecting my aunt had shared my story with him, feeling betrayed by her supposed confidentiality.

My frustration peaked as I defensively crossed my arms, inwardly renouncing the very people I was among. The shadows of my past started to mock me. Jeering at the audacity I had to sit amongst God's chosen. I didn't belong there. But then, the pastor called for the altar service, and the congregation flooded the altar, drawn by his compelling invitation. I sunk deeper into my chair, waiting for him to move on.

As the pastor continued his call, only a few remained seated among the congregation. His voice echoed through the church, "Come on, there's still someone here. You need to come forward. You need to give your life to Christ." I puzzled over his insistence, wondering, "What is he talking about?" Gradually, more attendees rose and moved towards the altar, leaving the pews nearly empty. As he persisted, calling and waiting, I felt the pressure of his gaze. To avoid being the last one seated, conspicuous and isolated, I reluctantly stood and approached the altar. The moment I did, he ceased his calls. "Now, they'll surely think it was me," I thought, a pang of self-consciousness washing over me. I navigated through the crowd to a quiet corner of the altar, feeling out of place and uncertain of what was expected next.

There I stood, observing the intense fervor around me. People were weeping openly, their cries filling the air; others were engaged in deep prayer or even jumping with joy. This entire scene was foreign to me. I was bewildered, having never witnessed such expressions of faith. Amidst this, a man approached and asked if he could pray for me. Somewhat indifferent, I agreed with a simple, "Okay, whatever." He placed his hands on me and started praying, urging me to speak out in another language. Confused, I thought, "What is he talking about? I only know one language." Yet, unexpectedly, a warm sensation overcame me, and words began to flow from me without understanding.

The next thing I knew, my aunt was beside me, her excitement palpable as my little cousins jumped around joyously. They exclaimed, "Do you want to get baptized? You spoke in tongues! You were filled with the Holy Ghost!" Their enthusiasm was overwhelming but I agreed to be baptized. "Why not? Let's go through with the entire experience," I thought, eager to conclude whatever had started.

We proceeded to the baptismal pool. There, I shed my former self; I confessed my sins and genuinely welcomed a new direction in life as I was submerged in the water. Emerging from the baptism, I felt as though a profound change had occurred within me, as if I had been truly renewed by the experience. This is where I began to *breathe* again.

Submerged and then raised from the water, I was transformed. The person who emerged was not the same as the one who had gone under. I felt a profound joy and clarity I had not known before. I felt changed. I felt different. I felt lighter. I felt happy. Everything was so bright. Did they turn on more lights? I was struck by how vivid everything appeared. It was as though I had been cleansed not just spiritually, but perceptually. I felt power flowing throughout my body. There was an overwhelming presence of authority and love that engulfed me. I was later able to identify the presence as the Lion of the tribe of Judah. I felt the strength and power of Jesus all at once but did not have the words to describe it. The Lion of Judah marked me as His own. My view of lions changed the day I was saved. I no longer saw the lion as a predator but as a protector. There was an immediate sense of belonging and a peace that reassured my once anxious mind.

After the ceremony, I redressed and exited the church amidst the congratulatory praises of the congregation. With a polite nod, I made my way to my car. Once inside the car, I instinctively reached for a blunt, lighting it up as I had done countless times before. I was dependent on that substance for years. I didn't know what it was to live without it. Within minutes, nausea overwhelmed me. Confused, I tossed it aside and tried another, only to be met with the same sickening feeling. "Something must be off with these," I thought, deciding to upgrade to a higher quality. Yet, even with the exotic blend, the result was the same: unbearable sickness.

Frustrated, I turned to alcohol, thinking it a safer refuge. But as I sipped, the familiar warmth of the buzz was soon replaced by an intense malaise. I managed to drive home and shared the news of my baptism with my mother. Almost immediately, I was gripped by a vertigo so severe I thought I might faint—a first for me, despite my years of heavy drinking.

Lying down, I was haunted by the realization that every attempt to smoke or drink repulsed my body. It was as if a divine intervention had rerouted my very desires. "What has God done to me?" I pondered, grappling with the loss of my old vices. The substances I had relied on to escape reality now repelled me, leaving me naked before the harsh truths of life. I wanted to retreat, to exist in my constructed fantasies where consequences were muted and reality was a distant echo. But without my substances, I was confronted with the stark necessity to truly live— and I was terrified of what that meant.

10

IMPOSTER AMONG BELIEVERS

As I embarked on my spiritual journey, a significant struggle emerged, one that wrestled with the deeply ingrained perceptions of Christianity I had carried from childhood. My earliest memories of the faith were filtered through the actions of my grandmother, who was a beacon of joy in her devotion. She returned from church radiant, her days marked by gospel songs and an evident love for God that she expressed even in her daily chores. To me, as a child who watched from the sidelines, her actions seemed overly pious and disconnected from the reality I knew. I recall the few times she brought me along to services—I felt so out of place, surrounded by rituals that meant nothing to me.

Yet, despite my reservations, my path led me back to the church's doors repeatedly after I got saved. It was as if a force beyond my comprehension was pulling me towards this new existence. Each Sunday, I returned, initially out of curiosity, then something more profound began to stir within me. The hymns of the choir moved me to tears, a reaction that puzzled and frustrated me. It was as though the music and the messages reached deep into my soul, awakening a torrent of buried emotions. I tried to suppress these feelings, maintaining a composed exterior to hide my vulnerability from the watchful eyes of the congregation.

However, the real battle ensued in solitude. Alone, I faced the stark contrast between my past and the life I was now pursuing. Memories of my old habits haunted me, as did thoughts of the relationships I had jeopardized for this newfound faith. I struggled to reconcile the person I had been with the one I was becoming. When faced with decisions about my relationships, particularly with a man I deeply cared for, I found myself at a crossroads. His willingness to join me at church, only to revert to our old ways afterward, forced a decisive action on my part. I had to end things, a choice that underscored the serious commitment I was making to my faith.

This internal conflict often left me feeling like an imposter among true believers. I questioned my place within the church, feeling alien and isolated despite the friendly faces around me. The more I engaged with the community, the more intense my inner turmoil became. I wrestled with the guilt of my past life and the overwhelming sense of not belonging, fearing that if people truly knew me, they would see the flaws I was desperately trying to overcome. I didn't realize yet that the enemy of my soul was at work. He did not want me to move in the power of God and kept accusing me to keep me bound. He attacked my identity, knowing my confidence was shaken. If he could keep me from seeing my true self through the eyes of God, then I would never become who God created me to be: a disruptor of hell.

Navigating this new world was a constant battle between the pull of my previous life and the call to something greater. Each step forward was weighed down by the echoes of my former self, challenging my resolve and forcing me to confront the reality of my transformation. This journey was not just about finding faith but also about redefining who I was in the light of that faith, a journey fraught with challenges but also illuminated by moments of profound personal revelation.

Continuing from my decision to cut ties with my past, the deeper

I delved into my church life, the more intense the internal conflict became. Attending church felt right; I was learning about God's teachings and His promises, absorbing what it meant to truly live as a Christian. However, each time I left the church, the stark contrast between my new environment and my old self became painfully evident. My mind was besieged with doubts and self-deprecation. The whispers were relentless, berating me with reminders of my past, insisting that no one would accept the real me—a person they perceived as tainted and unworthy.

This internal narrative of feeling like an outsider persisted. In public, I played the part well, performing the role of a faithful believer with a smile. Yet, in solitude, my old demons returned, mocking my efforts and dismissing the value of my spiritual journey. It was an internal battle that made me feel like I was on the losing side. The demons taunted me, calling it futile to seek transformation through a faith in a God I could not see. The shame was overwhelming. When others attempted to get closer, I recoiled, fearing their proximity would expose my imperfections and invite judgment and condemnation—something I already inflicted upon myself in abundance.

Unable to cope with the mounting pressure and cognitive dissonance, I relapsed into old habits for relief. I told myself that moderate drinking was acceptable if it helped keep the despair at bay. Yet, the more I drank, the more I needed to numb the persistent ache in my heart and quiet the tumultuous thoughts swirling in my mind. Soon, even alcohol wasn't enough to stifle the pain.

Driven by desperation, I revisited another old vice—smoking. Returning to my old suppliers, I was met with puzzlement; they hardly recognized me. I attributed it to my changed appearance— dresses and skirts. This marked me as different, although I felt unchanged at the core. Their questions and hesitant attitudes frustrated me, compelling me to seek out those who wouldn't question the contradictions of my appearance and actions. "I need stuff," I would insist, clinging to the familiarity of these transactions. They reluctantly provided what I sought, enabling me to retreat once again into a haze of smoke that I hoped would shield me from the reality of my struggles.

This return to my old ways, however, was not without its own set of challenges. Each session of self-medication was a testament to my ongoing battle—a clash between the life I was trying to leave behind and the new path I was struggling to forge. Despite the temporary escape, the reality of my situation was clear: I was trapped in a cycle of dependency and self-loathing, a far cry from the redemption and peace I sought through my faith.

Amidst this profound darkness, the desire to vanish from the world grew. I felt an overwhelming urge to end the suffering, to step out of a life that no longer made sense to me. The pain, the loneliness, and the sense of being perpetually lost were unbearable. I no longer wanted to be part of this world, feeling completely disconnected from everything and everyone. The despair was suffocating, and I found myself longing for an end, for a peace that seemed only achievable through the cessation of my existence.

11

FROM SHADOWS TO LIGHT

Several months had passed since I had embraced my new faith, and with each day, the community's warmth drew me deeper into church life. Despite my initial hesitation, the persistent invitations to join the choir became harder to ignore. I wasn't a singer—far from it—and I expressed this openly. Yet, they were relentless. The choir director's wife, along with my church sister, who had a motherly presence and served as the choir's secretary, extended heartfelt invitations. Their encouragement wasn't just about filling ranks in the choir; they saw something in me that I had yet to see in myself.

During this time, I felt particularly drawn to an elder in the church. His guidance seemed to come directly from a place of divine insight. He referred to me affectionately as "daughter," a term that resonated deeply, providing a sense of belonging I hadn't realized I was missing. His prophetic words during our conversations often left me contemplating deeper truths about my path and purpose. The connection felt ordained, a guiding light as I navigated my new reality.

One of the transformative moments came during a special prayer event at the church, our annual ten days of prayer. During one segment, we were to pray with someone for about two minutes before switching partners on a cue. This exercise, though initially outside my comfort zone, propelled me into a reflective and spiritually active engagement with my community.

Yielding to the gentle nudges from my new church family, I finally decided to attend a choir rehearsal just to observe. The welcoming atmosphere was undeniable. The choir members were not just friendly; they radiated a genuine enthusiasm that was contagious. It felt like fun, and it was engaging in a way that church had never been for me before. By the end of that first rehearsal, my reservations had melted away. I decided to join the choir, thinking it would at least give me something to do beyond the routine church services.

Joining the choir proved to be more than just a casual commitment. The songs we practiced, which once moved me to tears, began to stir a different emotion in me—gratitude. Singing became a cathartic release, and the lyrics ministered to me as much as they seemed to reach the hearts of the congregation. What began as a reluctant agreement to participate had blossomed into a profound channel for connection and ministry. I was not only receiving the messages in the music but also passing them on, resonating with the congregation in a way I had never anticipated.

Through music, I found a way to express the complex emotions that my journey of faith stirred within me. I felt like King Saul who was plagued by evil spirits needing the instrument of music to calm me. Each note sung was a step towards healing, a step towards embracing the fullness of my new life, and a step towards understanding the depth of grace that had been extended to me. In this choir, I was no longer just a voice among many; I had found my own voice, one that was powerful, healing, and deeply connected to the divine spirit of God that I was learning to trust more each day.

I began to find solace and expression in the choir; the deeper implications of my involvement became increasingly evident. The affirmations from congregation members, telling me how my worship touched them, initially caught me off guard. I hadn't realized the impact of my presence; I was simply absorbed in the music and the lyrics that echoed the sentiments of my heart. Gradually, I surrendered to the overwhelming sense of divine love that enveloped me during these moments of praise. It felt like a pure embrace from God, one that I clung to fervently, allowing myself to vanish into worship, disconnecting from the world to connect profoundly with the Father. Life breathed into me with every song I sang. It revived me and gave meaning to my life. The songs were not just words; they were healing balms to my wounds.

However, as more people shared how my worship appeared to them, describing a person who seemed so different from who I felt I was, I began to feel exposed and vulnerable. I would lose myself in praise and worship, enjoying an intimate time with just me and my protector, safe in His embrace. The words of the members painted a picture of a transformed individual, which conflicted with my self-perception. I was still trying to find my way through faith and learning who I was in Christ. I struggled to reconcile their image of me with my own identity. Despite the scriptural promise of renewal in Christ—that in Him, we are made new creatures with the past left behind—I lacked a deep understanding of these words. This lack of scriptural grounding made it difficult to accept the 'newness' others saw in me.

During this period of internal conflict, the elder who became a father figure to me, approached me with profound insight. He saw beyond my surface-level contributions to the praise team, recognizing a deeper calling within me. With a direct and purposeful manner, he spoke life into my doubts, declaring that I was an intercessor with a prophetic gift waiting to be fully realized and utilized. He urged me to step out of the shadows, to embrace the gifts God had placed within me, and to activate the potential he perceived so clearly.

As he prayed over me, I felt an overwhelming sense of God's presence, a weight that was both glorious and daunting. Tears flowed freely as I grappled with the enormity of what was being asked of me. Prayer seemed to follow me wherever I went. Doubts about my spiritual gifts, particularly intercession and prophecy, clouded my thoughts. I worried about my distinct way of praying, which didn't seem to fit the conventional modes I observed around me. The fear of praying publicly, of somehow being inadequate due to my past or different style, often left me feeling spiritually choked, as if a literal constriction prevented me from voicing my prayers. "How could this good God choose a wretch like me to go before his people?" I thought to myself.

Amidst these trials, the sermons at church began to focus on themes of forgiveness. The messages challenged me to confront my past and the people who had hurt me. This was a daunting task, as it not only involved forgiving others but also accepting that God's forgiveness extended to me as well. The notion that I needed to forgive as I had been forgiven was a profound call to let go of old grudges and pains that had long shaped my worldview. I believed that forgiveness should be earned. How can one forgive without receiving an apology from the offender?

The profound internal struggle I was experiencing intensified with the daunting task of forgiving those who had wronged me from my earliest memories. The notion of forgiveness as a path to personal peace was alien to me, even infuriating. My heart hardened against the idea, especially when the messages at church and inter-actions with church members seemed to push me towards what felt like an impossible reconciliation with my past. As these demands grew, so did my isolation; I withdrew from those around me, from those trying to guide and support me, because their expectations seemed so far removed from the reality of my pain and trauma. "They don't know about my ordeal. They don't know what i've been through. Why should I let these people off the hook? They knew better, but chose to be selfish and hurt me." I was blinded by the pain of betrayal. My healing was bound up in forgiveness, but I chose pain over praise.

As my emotional state deteriorated, reminders of my past began to intrude unexpectedly into my daily life. Encounters with individuals from my past—both men and women who had been part of the darkest chapters of my story—became frequent and distressing. Each sighting, each interaction, was a trigger, transporting me back to moments of profound pain and making me feel as though I was reliving those traumas. These experiences left me crippled, questioning the very identity I was trying to build in my new Christian life. Doubts about my future, about whether I truly belonged to this new path or if I should return to my old life, plagued me relentlessly. I desperately cried out to God for answers on who I was, and what He wanted from me.

Nightmares and flashbacks haunted both my nights and days. The constant mental torment felt inescapable, and the fear that the Christian community would reject me if they knew my entire story only deepened my crisis. I felt trapped between two worlds, neither of which seemed to offer a place where I could just be myself without judgment or fear. This led to a severe anxiety attack, a physical manifestation of the intense pressure and inner turmoil I was enduring.

In a moment of desperation, Holy Spirit led me to reach out to my elder from the church, someone who had shown wisdom and patience in the past. His calm demeanor was a small comfort as I unraveled, revealing the depth of my anxiety and confusion. Surprisingly, he asked about my father—a figure absent from my life and seemingly unrelated to my immediate struggles. Yet, this question unlocked a flood of emotions I hadn't realized were influencing my current state. As I cried uncontrollably, something within me began to shift.

My elder then asked me a pivotal question about my life story, prompting me to consider what part would be the easiest to write about. Without hesitation, I realized it would be the chapter about my journey with God—the point at which I truly began to live.

Acknowledging this was a profound moment of clarity. It was then I understood that my life with God marked the beginning of true existence, a life where past traumas no longer needed to define me. In Christ, I was not just surviving; I was truly alive.

This realization brought a newfound peace that enveloped me, soothing the tumult within. It marked a definitive turn in my journey, a point where I could start to see a way forward, not by forgetting my past but by not letting it control my future. In embracing my faith and the new life it offered, I found not just solace but a vibrant new beginning. This was the start of a completely renewed existence. I was crawling my way out of darkness towards the light of revelation. The Lion of the Tribe of Judah called me.

12

HEALED FOR REAL?

Discussing my past has always been a journey through darkness, a passage marked by pain and shadows. Much of my life's story has been burdened by negative experiences—only a fraction of which I've shared—but this chapter brings a shift towards something profoundly hopeful: my personal relationship with God.

This part of my journey is where I became intentional about my faith. No longer content with surface-level understanding, I dove deeply into scripture, seeking to truly know the God I had been worshiping in song and sermon. "God," I prayed with fervent desperation, "if I'm to walk this path genuinely, I need to know You for real." This wasn't just a desire for knowledge but a plea for a genuine encounter. I told God that without His real presence in my life, I might walk away forever, given how frequently I found myself slipping back into old, destructive patterns. Every step forward was met with relentless warfare. My relationships, finances, mental health, and physical health all took hits. It seemed as though an invisible force preferred to keep me in a pit of doom rather than allow me to stay afloat and truly live.

My plea was raw and unfiltered: I needed to experience God as a Father, a role I had never understood due to my own father's absence. The concept of a loving, protective parent was foreign, and yet, I was calling out for just that—to feel God's paternal love, guidance, and acceptance. This was a critical moment, a make-or-break point where my faith needed to become more than ritual—it needed to become my lifeline. I continued reading and studying the Word, as well as prayed daily, until I could discern that the Spirit of God was with me.

As I immersed myself more in worship music at home, I wasn't just listening—I was reaching out for a connection that went beyond words. One day, while cleaning my apartment, I was profoundly moved by a song called "Everything." The lyrics echoed through my space, declaring God as everything one could need—*Master, Savior, Redeemer, Deliverer*. The song ministered to me so deeply that I was compelled to stop cleaning. Overwhelmed by the Holy Spirit, I found myself on my knees, weeping and transitioning from singing in English to speaking in tongues. This spontaneous moment of spiritual release was unlike anything I had experienced; it was as if God Himself had stepped into my apartment to answer my desperate cries.

There, on my knees, with tears streaming down my face and divine words flowing from my lips, I encountered God's presence in the most intimate way. It was an affirmation that He was indeed real, responding to my call in the most personal and transformative manner. When I finally rose from the floor, my perspective had shifted dramatically. I felt renewed, as though I had been lifted from a pit of despair and set upon a new path illuminated by God's divine light.

This profound experience marked a turning point in my spiritual journey. No longer was I merely following the motions; I had met God in the solitude of my living room. This encounter didn't just change my understanding of faith; it revolutionized how I viewed myself and my place in the world. It was a clear message that despite my past and the doubts that haunted me, I was worthy of God's divine love and intervention. The path ahead remained fraught with challenges, but I now walked it with a profound sense of purpose and divine companionship, assured that God was with me, guiding each step of my transformative journey.

As I continued my journey, the profound personal encounter with God in my apartment was a pivotal moment that transformed my understanding of my worth and my relationship with God. Overwhelmed with joy and gratitude, I knew that God had not disqualified me; the feelings of being unclean and unworthy were projections of my own fears, not reflections of how God saw me. In that unforgettable moment of worship, alone yet deeply connected, I felt the divine presence of God affirming that I was heard, loved, and valued. It was a reassurance that no matter my past, I was not beyond the reach of God's grace.

This newfound connection spurred me to delve deeper into the Bible, starting from Genesis. I approached the scripture with a fresh zeal, eager to absorb every word and uncover the character of God as revealed through the Biblical narratives. The Old Testament stories painted a picture of a powerful, sovereign God, while the Gospels introduced me to Jesus's compassionate ministry. Through these texts, I discovered the relentless love and forgiveness of God, learning that nothing could separate me from His love. This realization was liberating; it dismantled the false notion of disqualification that had haunted me.

Reading the Bible became a journey of self-discovery. Each scripture reflected back to me not only God's character but also my own identity as seen through His eyes. I began to understand how much God loved me, a realization that slowly started to dismantle the strongholds of fear, condemnation, and incorrect thought patterns that had imprisoned me for so long. I actively worked to shift my focus towards thoughts that were good, lovely, and true—principles that brought life and healing to my mind and spirit.

The Book of John, in particular, was transformative for me.

John's portrayal of Jesus resonated deeply, making the Lord's presence feel even more real and tangible. The opening verses of John, which declare the Word's divine nature and creative power, were not just lines of scripture but a vivid, life-giving reality to me. "In the beginning was the Word, and the Word was with God, and the Word was God." These words were a revelation, illuminating the profound truth of Jesus's divinity and His active presence in my life. They reinforced my conviction that Jesus was indeed real, alive, and active in my existence.

As I immersed myself more in the scriptures, my ability to discern and hear God's voice improved. The conflicting voices of doubt and divine guidance that had once torn at my conscience began to resolve, tilting more towards clarity and truth. The 'angel' side, representing guidance and positivity, became more dominant, enabling me to discern better and navigate my thoughts and actions with greater wisdom.

This chapter of my spiritual journey was marked by dramatic growth and a deepening relationship with God. By engaging with His word, I wasn't just learning about God—I was meeting Him in the pages of scripture, and this interaction was reshaping my entire life. I emerged from this period not only more knowledgeable of Biblical teachings but profoundly changed, equipped with a stronger, clearer understanding of my path forward, rooted in the life-giving power of God's word.

As my spiritual journey deepened, the newfound clarity and connection with God also ushered in an evolution of my prayer life. No longer hesitant, I began to pray with a conviction and depth that sprang from the well of divine overflow within me. This transformation was not just about feeling closer to God but also understanding the distinction between genuine faith and religious formalism. I learned that religion, as a system of traditions and man-made rules, often distorted the pure essence of spiritual life by bending the very words and character of God. This revelation was both liberating and challenging, as it pushed me to reevaluate the way I expressed my faith, ensuring it was aligned with Biblical truth rather than mere religious routine.

God's gentle correction did not stop with altering my under-standing of religion; it also expanded into my dreams. Initially, my dreams were haunted by nightmares, a reflection of the unresolved traumas of my past. But as I engaged more deeply with scripture and allowed the Holy Spirit to work within me, the nature of my dreams shifted dramatically. They became vivid and prophetic, revealing not only future calamities but also visions of a renewed Earth—scenes of destruction followed by profound renewal and beauty. These dreams were both unsettling and awe-inspiring, filling me with a sense of both foreboding and hope.

One particular dream left a lasting impact. It began on a seem-ingly desolate train carrying lifeless bodies, symbolizing perhaps the death of my old fears and insecurities. The dream transitioned to a vibrant new world, where the freshness of creation and the joy of new beginnings were palpable. These visions, though symbolic, underscored the transformative work God was doing in my life—from death to life, from old to new.

This sequence of revelatory dreams did not just affect me; they started spilling over into my interactions with others. I began to share these visions with friends, family, and church members. Initially, my accounts were met with skepticism and surprise, but as the accuracy of these dreams became apparent, it was clear that God was using me to speak into the lives of others. This role as a dreamer and a voice to this generation was unexpected but deeply affirming. It was a testament to the fact that God had indeed heard my cries for authenticity in my walk with Him.

The accuracy of these dreams and the reactions they elicited from others often left me feeling bewildered, yet they also confirmed the unique path God was carving out for me. Each vision, each dream interpretation served as a stepping stone, guiding me and those around me toward deeper spiritual truths and understandings. Through these experiences, I learned that embracing my spiritual gifts was not just about personal transformation but also about contributing to the community's growth and well-being. It was about giving God the glory. This realization was both a challenge and an invitation to step fully into the roles God had prepared for me, embracing the new life He had promised—a life marked by divine encounters, prophetic insights, and the relentless pursuit of His presence.

As my spiritual journey progressed, the prophetic dreams I experienced began to create an unexpected tension between me and my friends. Their discomfort with the accuracy of the dreams I had concerning them led them to ask me not to share my visions with them. They were uncomfortable with the exposure of what I saw and heard. This reaction was painful; I felt rejected by those close to me, isolated because of a gift I was only beginning to understand. However, I soon realized that these revelations were not always meant for disclosure. Sometimes, God showed me things not to expose or confront others, but to intercede for them in prayer. Learning to discern whether to speak or to remain silent was a crucial lesson in my spiritual development, one that brought a deeper understanding of my role as an intercessor.

This sense of separation from others, coupled with my emerging gifts and intercessory prayer, often made me feel like an outcast once again. A familiar territory I knew since childhood. Doubts crept back in, and I questioned my place within the church and even my sanity. During this period of confusion, I attended a concert to support a friend and encountered a moment of divine instruction that I initially resisted. Overwhelmed by the fear of being misunderstood, I wanted to avoid speaking out. Yet, as I attempted to leave, a physical sensation of heaviness made it impossible to move, compelling me to interact with one of the performers, a woman who turned out to be deeply in need of encouragement.

The encounter did not end at the concert. I later met the same woman at another event where I was working as a photographer. She recognized me and not only hired me on the spot but also provided profound spiritual counsel. She urged me to "turn off the noise," the lies and doubts seeded by the enemy, and to focus on the truth of God's word and my calling. Her advice was a revelation, highlighting the importance of guarding my thoughts and focusing on God's affirmations rather than the enemy's deceptions.

Following this advice, I began to experience divine appointments in everyday settings—from grocery stores to fast food lines—where I was led to perform random acts of kindness. These acts often opened doors for meaningful exchanges where others would share their stories or speak words of encouragement into my life. Despite my initial discomfort with receiving recognition, these moments taught me the value of accepting affirmation as part of embracing my identity in Christ.

Each of these interactions was a lesson in the broader, divine orchestration of my life. They taught me that my spiritual gifts were not just for personal edification but were meant to bless others in tangible and intangible ways. Through these experiences, I gradually learned to embrace my role within the body of Christ more fully, understanding that each act of faith, no matter how small, was part of a larger tapestry of God's work in and through me. This journey of acceptance and active participation marked a significant evolution in my faith, teaching me that living out one's faith authentically involves not just understanding one's gifts but actively using them in service to others and to God's greater glory.

In my spiritual journey, akin to Jonah, I often found myself wearing my "Jonah sneakers," running in the opposite direction from where God was leading me. During this tumultuous period, filled with doubts about my sanity and the authenticity of my prophetic experiences, I found myself constantly resisting God's pull towards deeper healing. I was adamant about leaving my past behind, convinced that revisiting old wounds was unnecessary and potentially destructive. "Leave me alone, Lord. I ain't going there," became my refrain as I struggled against God's persistent call to confront and heal from my past. I wanted to pretend my past didn't affect my present. I tried to push it out of my mind as if it was not even me that went through the traumas. I was trying to lead while bleeding all over the place, all the while broken and hurting, trapped from the first offense.

This resistance culminated at a conference I attended somewhat reluctantly. The event was titled "Healed for Real," a theme that I would have avoided had I known ahead of time. As I sat in the audience, my discomfort grew; the preacher's words pierced through my defenses, and the title displayed on the screen only intensified my urge to flee. My friend and I planned our escape, waiting for just the right moment to slip out unnoticed.

However, before we could enact our plan, the pastor, also known as the Dr. of Souls, singled me out from the pulpit. Her direct approach and insistence that we speak after her sermon felt like a confrontation I was not prepared for. My initial reaction was one of defiance and disbelief, but as she approached me, the entire congregation's eyes were on me, making it impossible to hide or run away. I felt the rage boiling within me. She had no right to single me out. I couldn't fathom why she would then approach me in the midst of her sermon. I wanted to leave, but there was no escape. I felt trapped.

The pastor stood before me and asked for an embrace. Reluctantly, I stood and allowed her to do as she asked. This hug, unexpected and powerful, broke through all my defenses. It was as if she physically pulled away chains that had long been wrapped tightly around my spirit. In her arms, I found myself overwhelmed with emotion, crying uncontrollably for every hurt I had ever experienced. This was not just crying; it was a cathartic release of every trauma, every violation, and every silenced scream from my past. Her embrace reached deep into my soul, touching the wounds of the little girl within me who had suffered so much.

In that moment, all the walls I had built, all the running and hiding, came to an abrupt end. I was exposed, vulnerable, and raw in the arms of a woman who God used to initiate profound healing in my life. The embrace felt like a divine intervention, a breaking and a making that was necessary for my journey forward. As the pastor released me from the hug, she wiped away my tears and asked to speak with me later, leaving me to process the profound shift that had just occurred.

This experience marked a significant turning point in my journey. It was at this conference, in the unexpected and divinely orchestrated embrace, that I began to truly understand the depth of God's love and His desire for my complete healing. The walls I had built to protect myself from the pain of my past were dismantled, not to expose and shame me, but to free me and rebuild me in the image of the healed, whole person God intended me to be.

As I stayed through the end of the message, now no longer planning to flee, I realized that healing was not just about confronting past pains but about allowing God to renew and transform every broken place. This "Healed for Real" moment wasn't just about physical presence at a conference; it was about a spiritual realignment and a commitment to walk the path of healing, no matter how challenging the journey might be. This embrace did not just break me; it also began the process of remaking me, setting the stage for a deeper, more authentic walk with God where I could truly live out my faith healed and whole.

13
THE HIGHER CALLING

After the transformative embrace at the conference, which left deep imprints on my soul, I exchanged numbers with one of the pastors, as requested by her. As the conference ended, I stood with a friend at the pier, gazing out over the expansive body of water. This moment, immersed in the natural beauty and calm of the waters, mirrored the tumultuous emotions swirling within me. It was a confrontation of my past with my present, a moment where the depth of my experiences seemed to crash over me like waves from a great height.

Feeling overwhelmed, I sought solace where I often found it—in the grandeur of nature which, by comparison, rendered my problems insignificant and highlighted the greatness of God. This setting was a crucial reminder of my smallness in the grand scheme of things, and it momentarily helped shift my perspective and soothe the emotional turmoil.

However, the old habits, deeply ingrained, soon resurfaced. Vulnerability felt like an open wound, and in response, I reverted to my old ways of coping. Despite the strides I had made, the instinct to escape my feelings proved strong. I found myself reaching out to a male friend, seeking to numb my burgeoning emotions through familiar, yet destructive means. It was a relapse into old patterns, a retreat from the progress I had fought so hard to achieve.

In this state of conflict, I returned to church, a place I cherished for the anonymity it provided regarding my past. The congregation knew nothing of the battles I had fought—of the sexual assaults, the drug abuse, or the alcoholism that I never named but lived through. Church was a sanctuary, but also a stage where I played a part that felt increasingly inauthentic.

During a service, an unexpected event occurred. A prophet from South Africa with a commanding presence and a thick accent, visited our church. His reputation preceded him, and I was curious yet skeptical about what he might contribute to our congregation. His message was anticipated to be powerful, yet nothing prepared me for the personal acknowledgment I would receive. When the prophet called out my full name from the pulpit, a chill ran down my spine. How could a stranger, a man I had never met, know me so intimately? It was both unsettling and awe-inspiring.

Frozen in my seat, surrounded by familiar faces who now turned to look at me, I felt the full weight of his call. It was as if time had stopped, and in that moment, every doubt, every fear, and every piece of my guarded self felt exposed under the gaze of this man of God. The shock of being so personally and accurately identified by someone from halfway across the world was a stark reminder of God's divine watch over my life.

This encounter marked a profound realization: I was known, not just by the people in my immediate surroundings but by God Himself. It shattered any illusions of anonymity and forced me to confront the reality that I could not hide from God. No longer could I shield my past or my struggles from the God who clearly saw me, knew me, and still reached out to me with a call that was both personal and piercing.

The path forward was clear, yet daunting. I needed to align more closely with God, to study His word, and to fully embrace the identity He had for me—beyond the shadows of my former self. This chapter in my life was about acknowledging that while the waters of my past were tumultuous, they also held the reflection of a future filled with hope, healing, and divine revelation.

After the prophet correctly called and spelled my name during the church service, I was nudged forward by a familiar face from the congregation, which prompted me to step out of my comfort zone. The moment I walked towards the pulpit, enveloped by a mix of awe and anxiety, I was acutely aware of every eye in the congregation. Despite the prophet speaking directly to me, my nerves drowned out his words; my heart raced, my palms sweated, and a sense of being underwater washed over me, blurring the rest of the experience into a haze.

Reflecting on this profound encounter, I realized the depth of God's awareness and care for me. It was a powerful affirmation that God not only sees but actively reaches out to us, even from across continents, through His servants. This realization was both humbling and elevating, pushing me to recommit to understanding God's word and presence in my life more deeply.

This deepened commitment to my faith was soon tested. Weeks later, during a routine church service, an announcement was made that startled me. My name was called along with others to meet at the altar post-service. The reason? We were being initiated as ministers in training. The shock of this announcement rooted me to the spot. Doubts flooded my mind—I was overwhelmed by a sense of unworthiness and disbelief. How could I, with my tumultuous past and ongoing internal battles, serve as a minister? I felt utterly unprepared and inadequate for such a responsibility.

At the altar, as the elder congratulated us, I was silent but internally chaotic, planning to dispute this decision. However, before I could express my concerns, another individual openly questioned the decision, echoing my internal turmoil. This moment at the altar was a crossroads, confronting me with the reality of my new identity in the church—an identity that seemed at odds with the image I had of myself.

This chapter in my journey underscored a crucial lesson: God's call does not wait for us to feel ready or worthy. It often comes when we are most aware of our flaws and least confident in our abilities. The call to ministry was not a mistake but a divine challenge to embrace a higher purpose beyond my self-doubts and past.

As I wrestled with this new role, I was forced to confront my self-image and the discrepancies between how I saw myself and how God saw me. This period was marked by intense personal growth and the daunting task of aligning my perception with God's vision for me. The journey was not just about accepting a title but about transforming into someone who could genuinely embody that role, supported by faith and a deeper understanding of God's unconditional love and purpose. I felt led to meet with my pastor to be open and honest with him. Thankfully, he made himself available to hear what I had to say.

God revealed to me that I didn't truly know Him as a Father. As I spoke, the pastor listened intently. He didn't interrupt, he didn't judge; he simply allowed me to share the raw and tumultuous emotions that had overwhelmed me. As I poured out my revelations and confessions, my pastor's response was one of understanding and compassion. He encouraged me, reminding me that this journey with God is a continual process of learning and unlearning, of breaking down and building up.

He shared his own experiences, emphasizing that these feelings were common among many who are called into ministry. He reassured me that God doesn't call the equipped; He equips the called. This resonated deeply with me, as it dismantled the daunting expectations I had set for myself. My pastor's words were a balm to my anxious spirit, and he prayed with me, asking God to strengthen my faith and to solidify my understanding of His fatherly love.

Leaving my pastor's office, I felt a significant shift within me. I realized that the title of minister was not just about preaching or leading a congregation, but about being willing to serve God and grow in His love, regardless of my past or how I perceived myself. It was about allowing God to use my life as a testament to His transforming power.

This encounter marked a pivotal chapter in my spiritual journey. I began to embrace the responsibilities of ministry not as burdens, but as opportunities to witness and to participate in the work God was doing in and through me. I dove deeper into my theological studies, not just to fulfill the requirements of the training but to truly understand the heart of God and His Word.

As the date of the ordination approached, anxiety almost knocked me out. I questioned myself and the choice the church made concerning me. The accuser of the brethren tormented me by presenting my past before me. I had a moment of weakness and decided I would not show up for the ordination because I was not truly qualified. I heard a roar in my ear that made one statement. The voice of many waters, in a firm yet calm voice, said, "I chose you." I hurriedly got dressed in my vestments and quickly left for church. My apprehension transformed into anticipation. Surrounded by fellow ministers in training, I found a community of support. Each of us was wrestling with our own insecurities and imperfections but buoyed by a common purpose. We learned together, prayed together, and grew together, each step taking us closer to a deeper communion with God.

On the day of the ordination, standing before the congregation, I felt a profound sense of humility and gratitude. The journey to this moment had been fraught with doubts and challenges, but also filled with undeniable encounters with God's grace. As I took the vows of ministry, I committed not just to serve but to continue seeking God's face, to be led by His Spirit, and to live out the calling He had placed on my life, one day at a time.

This chapter of my life, fraught with emotional upheavals and divine interventions, had led me to a place of purpose, deeply rooted in the knowledge that I am God's child, called and cherished, equipped by His grace to walk the path laid out for me. I was chosen by a good God to do the work of the kingdom.

One evening, during a small group meeting, I shared my story of finding refuge in Psalm 91. The responses were varied—some nodded in understanding, others offered hugs, but all showed a level of empathy that I hadn't expected. They didn't see the broken, unworthy person I feared I was; they saw a fellow believer finding their way back to God's heart, a journey they too were familiar with.

This community became a crucial part of my healing process. They were living proof that while my past was a part of me, it didn't define me. My identity was not in the brokenness I felt but in the wholeness offered through Christ. Their presence reminded me that the church was not just a place of judgment but a place of grace and growth.

Despite having good times, I sometimes struggled. I would tend to fall into a deep, dark place of depression. In the throes of profound depression, I found myself constantly withdrawing from those around me. Beneath the surface, I battled a ceaseless turmoil—feeling utterly undeserving of any peace or joy. My fears were not of being disliked, but of being truly seen and consequently abandoned. Each accolade about my strength or my supposed closeness to God only deepened my fear of inevitable exposure as a fraud. The enemy is an accuser of the brethren, and he knew how to use my past to break me down. With every level I rose, he would show up to kick me back down.

I was caught in a vicious cycle of self-isolation, convinced that any intimacy would lead to rejection and disgrace. Despite appearances, inside I was crumbling—my smiles were masks, and my confidence a façade. Each interaction left me drained, fearing that my carefully constructed exterior might crumble at any moment.

So, I walked the thin line, the line between life and death, the line of pretense where I spent my days. There, I knew how to cry. I wept, relentlessly, because breaking free from the shackles that bound my spirit seemed an insurmountable task. Each night brought its own set of trials, and in my dreams, I was both captive and captive audience to messages and visions that transcended ordinary understanding. These were not mere dreams; they were communications, spiritual engagements that required me to write, to document—turning me into a scribe of my own supernatural experiences.

Night after night, the ritual was the same. I would open my Bible, intent on conquering it from Genesis to Revelation. Each attempt to read through the Bible had started with enthusiasm but fizzled out under the weight of routine. Yet, this time was different. I was determined to see it through, to not let the familiar cycle of restarts deter my progress. As I read deeper into the New Testament, fatigue overtook me, and I fell asleep with the Bible open, a silent sentinel by my side.

It was in this vulnerable state, half-lost in sleep, that I first heard it—the audible voice of God. It wasn't frightening; instead, it was like the rumble of many rivers or a gentle quake beneath the earth, resonant and full of an ancient power. He called me by name, simply, "Jaun." I sat up, startled yet unafraid, searching the dark corners of my room for an intruder who was not there.

With the realization that no one else was home, I felt an unmistakable pull back to the scripture. The voice was clear, encouraging me to continue reading. So I did. I returned to my Bible, picking up where I had left off, each word now infused with a new sense of purpose and connection.

This moment echoed the Biblical story of Samuel, who heard his name called in the night. Like him, it took me a few encounters to understand that it was not a person but God reaching out to me. If only I had known to respond, "Here I am, Lord," sooner, to acknowledge His presence and affirm my readiness to listen. He was calling me higher.

From then on, my journey through the Bible was not just about reading words; it was about engaging in a dialogue with God. I shared my insights with others, though not always to their delight. Many were indifferent, some even annoyed, thinking I had become too consumed with spirituality. They warned me of being "too heavenly minded to be of any earthly good," but I knew that if God is spirit, then being spiritual was not just good; it was necessary.

Despite the mixed reactions, I continued to share my revelations, primarily through social media. It was a platform that allowed me to express my thoughts without the immediate backlash or disinterest I often faced in person. The feedback was positive, sometimes profoundly so, with people reaching out to tell me how timely and impactful my words had been for them.

This encouragement led me to a deeper practice of prayer, what I came to understand as "pressing into prayer." This wasn't just routine prayer; it was a battle against distractions, against every thought that sought to pull me away from communion with God. I learned to counter each intrusive thought with scripture, reinforcing my focus and deepening my connection to God.

As I pressed on, my ability to hear God's voice amidst the noise of everyday life sharpened. I became adept at tuning out distractions, at focusing my mind and spirit on what was truly important. This practice didn't just enhance my prayer life; it transformed it, making each session a profound encounter with the divine.

My lessons were clear: the path to understanding and spiritual depth was through perseverance in reading the Word, through engaging with God not just in thought but in practice, and through sharing those insights with a world that might not always understand but desperately needs that connection. It was a path marked by trials, but also by tremendous growth—a journey of becoming not just a listener but a doer of the Word.

14

UNHEALTHY CYCLES

As I ponder the journey thus far, I recognize this chapter of my life as the warfare surrounding my "Yes" to a higher calling, a narrative intertwined with the theme of being "thrown in the pit," a concept I grapple to fully understand. The battles I face are not just spiritual or personal but deeply familial, impacting those I hold dear.

Since childhood, I harbored a belief in the inherent goodness of life, shielded from the realities of loss and death by the innocence of youth and the vibrant presence of my grandmother. Her home was the heart of our family, a place where Sundays were marked by laughter-filled gatherings, where cousins played and siblings bonded. These memories, so vivid and warm, are among the most cherished of my early years.

However, my grandmother's passing marked a turning point. Her death was not just a personal loss but a fissure through the center of our family life. The gatherings became sparse; the closeness we took for granted dissipated as each member dealt with their grief in solitude. It was as though her passing unraveled the tightly knit fabric of our family, leaving us isolated in our coping.

Years later, as I found myself in a new country, forging an identity anchored in my faith rather than the world I left behind, the
challenges persisted. I was constantly battling the urge to quit,
striving each day to live out my faith authentically. During this
period, tragedy struck again—my aunt, whom I had always known
and loved like a mother, succumbed to her long standing battle with
sickle cell anemia. Her death was a blow that pushed our family
further apart, as unresolved issues from the past surfaced, fueling
bitterness and facilitating our drift apart.

The geographical distance between us, with most of my family in
Jamaica and me in the United States, compounded the emotional
distance. Though we loved each other, our interactions were infre-
quent, reduced to necessary communications rather than the affec-
tionate, everyday interactions that characterize close familial
relationships.

Following my aunt's death, our family seemed to be caught in a
relentless cycle of loss. Death became a shadow that loomed persis-
tently over us, leading me to wonder if we were under a generational
curse. This series of losses drove me to seek solace and answers in
scripture. I found comfort in the promises of faith and the assurance
of eternal life for those in Christ. This prompted a fervent prayer
campaign for my family's salvation—that they might know Christ
and find healing, both physically and spiritually.

My faith became the lens through which I viewed these trials, a
framework that gave me hope and a path to advocate for my family's
spiritual well-being. However, the death of my grandfather was
another profound loss that tested this framework. His passing not
only marked the end of having living grandparents but also left a
void in the lives of his children, my mother and her siblings, who
now faced the world without the guidance of either parent.

This period of intense loss and spiritual warfare shaped my
resolve to deepen my faith and understanding of God's word. It was
during this time that I experienced profound spiritual revelations.
While delving into scripture, I heard the audible voice of God for the

first time, a voice that did not bring fear but clarity and direction. This divine encounter urged me to continue my scriptural studies and reinforced my commitment to intercede for my family.

Through these trials, I learned the power of prayer not just as a petition but as a transformative practice that could bring peace and focus amidst chaos. This realization led me to embrace my role as an intercessor, someone who stands in the gap, praying fervently for others' needs while navigating the complexities of personal and family challenges.

The relentless cycle of sin and repentance seemed to be an endless spiral, where each misstep heavily burdened my conscience and led me to question the genuineness of my faith and my capacity for true transformation.

Despite the turmoil within, my commitment to praying for my family never wavered. I believed firmly that through Christ, not only was personal transformation achievable, but healing for my loved ones was possible as well. This period was marked by personal struggles against my failures while simultaneously interceding for others, a dual battle that tested my faith deeply. Nonetheless, I clung to the hope of redemption and breaking free from the generational curses that seemed to ensnare my family.

My involvement in the church and a deeper commitment to spiritual growth provided a foundation of stability and purpose. Participating more fully in the prophetic ministry, I found solace and strength in our collective worship and the shared faith within our community. These moments of prayer and song offered brief periods of clarity and peace amidst the inner conflict.

However, this peace was transient. The enemy's tactics were sly and persistent, always ready to exploit a moment of weakness to dredge up past failures. Engaging in this spiritual warfare was grueling—a constant tug-of-war between the desires of the flesh and the aspirations of the spirit. The words of 1 Peter 5:8 echoed in my mind as a grim reminder: "Be sober, be vigilant; because your adversary the devil walks about like a roaring lion, seeking whom he may devour." This scripture underlined the necessity for vigilance in my spiritual walk, a path laden with challenges and the devil's relentless assaults.

Despite the ongoing struggles, my dedication to my faith remained unshaken. Each step forward was a testament to God's persistent grace and mercy. My prayers intensified, becoming more deliberate as I sought not only personal relief but also divine intervention for my family. I held a deep conviction in the transformative power of prayer to sever the bonds of illness and mortality that had long plagued us.

As I served in my ministerial role, the importance of being open and honest about my spiritual journey became increasingly clear. Discussing my challenges with trusted mentors in the church illuminated the fact that I was not alone in this fight. Their guidance and the accountability they offered were instrumental in helping me navigate this intricate journey.

The contrast between my public service and private struggles led me to a deeper appreciation of grace. It was not about achieving perfection, but about the willingness to face my flaws and surrender them to God. This acknowledgment brought a new depth of humility and reinforced my resolve to authentically live out my faith, recognizing my weaknesses while embracing the transformative power of God's love.

As I endeavored to live out my faith authentically, I found myself repeatedly succumbing to temptations that I thought I had overcome. This pattern of falling into sexual sin left me feeling increasingly despondent, questioning the validity and power of my faith. Why, despite my active ministry and the clear impact of my spiritual work on others, did I find myself trapped in this cycle of sin and redemption?

The pain of recurring failure was compounded by the palpable disintegration of my family ties, marked by successive losses and the residual grief that each death brought. It felt as though an insidious force was methodically working to undermine the foundational bonds that held my family together. In my desperation, I cried out to God to arrest this cycle of death, to spare my family from further pain. My prayers became declarations, commanding the spirit of illness to release its grip on my lineage. I stood firm in the belief that through divine intervention, the tide would turn.

During this turbulent period, my mother's struggle with my transformation became another layer of conflict. While she initially rejoiced at my baptism, my deeper involvement in church activities soon became a point of contention. She had hoped for a moderate change, one that would steer me away from destructive behaviors without leading to what she perceived as excessive religiosity. This misunderstanding highlighted the complex dynamics of faith within family relationships, where expectations can sometimes clash with personal spiritual journeys.

Amid these personal and familial challenges, I experienced a profound moment of vulnerability that forced me to confront my past traumas directly. A spiritual mentor in my church noticed my distress and approached me, offering a listening ear and a comforting presence. Her intervention led me to reveal the abuses I had suffered, starting from a very young age—a revelation that I had long suppressed. This disclosure was met with shock and concern, and ultimately led to the painful but necessary confrontation with my mother about my past.

This confrontation did not go as hoped. The family's reaction was one of disbelief and denial, primarily because the accused was a beloved family member. This response only deepened my sense of isolation and betrayal, intensifying my internal conflicts and pushing me further into despair. The lack of support and acknowledgment from my family made me question my worth and reality, leaving me to grapple with the heavy burden of unresolved trauma alone.

However, a pivotal encounter at a church event provided a turning point. A prophet's affirmation of my experiences and his assurance that I was not delusional reignited a spark of hope within me. His words, confirming the reality of my past and the presence of divine awareness and concern, helped me start to reclaim my sense of sanity and purpose. It was a moment of profound spiritual affirmation that restored my faith in God's omniscience and compassion.

This renewal of faith empowered me to recommit to my spiritual path, despite the ongoing challenges and the skepticism I faced from those around me. Every attempt to share the goodness of God was met with resistance, mirroring the Biblical account of Jonah, who fled from his divine mission only to find himself in the belly of a great fish. Like Jonah, I felt swallowed by darkness and despair, yet it was in this place of total surrender that I finally heard God's call anew.

Emerging from this metaphorical belly of the fish, I resolved to answer God's call without hesitation. This decision marked a new beginning in my spiritual journey, one characterized by a deeper commitment to obedience and a readiness to embrace the challenges of my divine calling. As I stepped forward to fulfill my role in the church and the broader community, I did so with a renewed sense of purpose and a heart fortified by divine grace and perseverance.

15

IN THE SHADOWS OF
ABSENCE

As I reflect on the profound moments that have shaped my journey, I recall the video I made about my father—a crucial narrative that sparked both healing and contention within me. It was in a previous chapter where I discussed an encounter with God on a mountain, a moment where He revealed to me that my inability to recognize Him as a father was hindering my acceptance of spiritual authority figures in my life, such as my pastor who later became my bishop. This revelation about fatherhood, both divine and earthly, set the stage for Chapter 16, where I delve deeper into the complexities of these relationships.

My earthly father's absence had a subtle yet profound effect on my life, a void that I only began to truly acknowledge during moments of deep reflection. It influenced my interactions with men, where past traumas colored every relationship, preventing me from forming healthy connections. My bishop's embrace, after a heartfelt conversation about what God had revealed concerning fatherhood, was a significant step towards healing, yet the absence of my biological father lingered like a shadow.

Father's Day at church brought this issue into sharper focus.

Celebrating fatherhood amidst a congregation where children rejoiced in their fathers' presence starkly contrasted with my own experiences. Discussions with others who lacked a father figure echoed my sentiments, highlighting a common void despite the presence of other paternal influences in our lives.

My inquiries about my father to my mother revealed his intermittent involvement in my early life, yet his reasons for not being present remained shrouded in mystery. This lack of presence led me to question not just his absence but the very nature of our potential relationship. Had he desired to be a part of my life, surely he would have made an effort.

A prophetess' conference, which I attended virtually, became a turning point. Connecting with her after being moved by the message of deliverance, I shared my experiences, which led to an invitation to contribute to a collaborative book project titled *50 Shades of Pink: The Journey to Self-Discovery*. This opportunity to write felt like divine timing, aligning with what God gave me to do as well as previous prophecies about my potential to impact others through writing.

Yet, the process was not without its challenges. Writing my story was a cathartic but tumultuous experience, as each word penned brought with it a resurgence of old wounds and confrontations with deeply buried truths. The reception of my contribution, while largely positive, also unveiled new layers of spiritual warfare and personal attacks, especially from those closest to me.

In the midst of this, a stark realization dawned on me: the enemy was not merely opposing me, but actively seeking to silence the transformative power of my testimony. Each step forward in faith was countered by efforts to drag me back into silence and despair.

But the words of a prophet at a church event confirmed what God spoke into my hearing, reaffirming my sanity and the reality of my experiences. His assurance that I was not alone, that I was seen and understood by God, reignited my will to fight against the darkness that sought to engulf me.

In this chapter of my life, the battles were fierce, the wounds deep, but the path to healing became clearer. Each challenge, each setback, each moment of validation served as a stepping stone towards a deeper understanding of my purpose and the transformative power of sharing one's truth. Through the pain, through the revelations, I found strength—not just to survive, but to thrive, fortified by a renewed faith in God's unwavering presence and the inevitable victory over the trials that tested my spirit.

16

THE TRUTH

This phase of my life marks a pivotal moment in my journey, as I face and own my truth. This crucial turning point wouldn't have been possible without the connections orchestrated by God, particularly through anointed and powerful individuals who have profoundly influenced my spiritual walk and personal healing. They were members of my congregation and people whom God sent to me in a season when I needed them.

During this time, I had a life-changing encounter with God at the altar of my church. I felt a strong calling from the Holy Spirit to approach the altar and humbly submit myself before God. With tears streaming down my face, I poured out my heart to Him, expressing my deep desire to know Him intimately, to hear His voice clearly, and to walk in His light. At that moment of repentance, I surrendered everything within me that did not reflect Him. I repented of my sins and made a sincere commitment to follow Him wholeheartedly.

At the altar, I stripped away all pretense and became completely vulnerable. I let my guard down, allowing God to touch me in the deepest parts of my being. I felt a stirring in my stomach, and before

I could utter another word, God began to release everything that had defiled me. Right there on the altar, I let go of all that was holding me back, and true deliverance took place.

When I rose from the altar, I felt a renewed sense of brightness and lightness, similar to the day I was baptized in Jesus' name. It was as if I could soar and fly out of the Tabernacle, overcome with joy and gratitude. I thanked God for hearing me, for answering my prayers, and for His unfailing love that never rejected me.

From that moment forward, my life took a dramatic turn. I walked in the newness of life, closely following God's guidance. He revealed Himself to me at the altar, and I responded by repenting and dedicating my life to serving Him wholeheartedly.

My journey has taught me that God's word is unyielding—it does not return void but accomplishes what it sets out to do. The power of this word pulled me from the depths of despair, saved me from near-fatal accidents, and kept me from taking my own life during my lowest moments. It's the word that has kept me rooted in the church, despite the relentless assaults of the enemy.

I've come to understand the importance of sharing my story, not just for my healing but to aid others who might be suffering in silence. The enemy wants us to believe that we are alone in our struggles—that our pains are unique and insurmountable. But this is a deception designed to isolate and weaken us. The truth is, we are never truly alone. God strategically places people in our lives to offer support and prayer, creating a network of care that sustains us through our trials.

This chapter of my life is about liberation—the shedding of false-hoods that shackle us and embracing the liberating truths of God's promises. It's about realizing that what happened to me does not define me; these experiences are merely things that happened but are not the sum total of who I am.

As I continue to say "Yes" to God, to walk with Him and trust in His path, I find strength and resolve. Each yes is a step away from my past and a step towards a future crafted by divine hands. Despite the fears and challenges that come with facing the unknown and the discomfort of growth, I am committed to moving forward, propelled by faith.

If it had not been for the Lord who was on my side, I would have been dead a long time ago. The Lion from the tribe of Judah stepped into my life and gave me the strength to stand. Through Him, I was able to breathe again; I found my voice to roar in the face of my enemy. I found a reason to praise beyond how I felt, and victory was won.

Now here I am, 16 years saved. When they say you have to work out your own salvation with fear and trembling, I didn't know it would mean having to fight to live. You're in the fight of your life because there's no good thing in this flesh, and as long as we are in this body, we have to make sure we die daily to ourselves.

As I matured in the faith, I have learned how to embrace God and His people all the more. I have learned to study the Word of God and apply it to my life, using it as my weapon against the enemy. The enemy will still come and try to kill and destroy what God has built in my life, but I know that life and death are in the power of my tongue. I will not fall to his tricks but keep my eyes lifted unto God in obedience, declaring the promises He has made for me.

His plans are to prosper me, not to harm me, to give me hope and a future. So, the best thing that I could have ever done was choose to walk with the Lion from the tribe of Judah. He is all-powerful, all-knowing, and all-seeing, full of grace. He has all authority, and as His child, I too walk in that same power and grace, knowing that no weapon formed against me shall prosper and every tongue that rises against me shall be condemned. It is my inheritance, and I live it.

I serve in ministry, something I wasn't comfortable doing, but the Lord dealt with me, and I was able to make a quick switch. Now, I love to serve God and His people. I love to work in the vineyard. To get to this point, I sought out a therapist. I remember her asking me,

"What is your greatest fear?" I immediately wanted to say I have no fear because I have the love of God, and perfect love casts out fear, but instead, I heard myself say, "I'm afraid to fail God." She asked, "Well, how can you fail God?" I responded by saying, "By not becoming." She had never heard anyone respond like that, and she was blown away by it, but it was truly my heart's cry. My desire is to hear, "Well done, thy good and faithful servant."

Many people have their own stories; some are like mine, some are worse than mine. Some don't come close, but through it all, God keeps sending them my way because He knows that I was able to overcome some of the most difficult things. And because I also know the true power and love of being grounded and rooted in God, that He saves and delivers. You don't have to be broken; I'm able to share with others that God has us all in His hands. We are just waiting to be mended and molded back together piece by piece, and when He finishes with us, we won't even have the look of a fracture.

Your life will be made whole. So, my desire moving forward in ministry is to ensure that everyone knows that God loves them, and that He just wants to put us together piece by piece to make us whole so we can live the abundant life. I want to mentor those who feel alone and lost in this world. I want them to come into who they truly are, into their identity in God, and be free. I know what God has done in my life, and I know He's done it time and again with others. If I could just encourage one person so that they can pass it on to another person, by the time He returns, we'll have millions of people who have testified of the glory of God working in their lives.

God is not coming back for a sick body; we must be restored. There are so many people who will come into the church looking different than what we're used to, hungry for God. I desire to be ready to receive them and lead them to Christ. This readiness is part of a larger journey that extends beyond merely overcoming obstacles —it involves transforming our pain into a purposeful existence. In doing so, I use my testimony to shatter the silence that often surrounds suffering and to challenge the lies of the enemy. My story underscores God's enduring faithfulness and His unwavering love— a love that empowers us to rise, to rebuild, and to renew our commitment to living fully in His grace. This is my testimony, my truth, and the foundation upon which I will build the rest of my life.

17
BEYOND THE SHADOWS OF THE PIT

As the end of our journey together nears, I am reminded of the Word of God from Romans 8:18, which states, "For I reckon that the sufferings of this present time are not worthy to be compared with the glory which shall be revealed in us." This scripture has been a beacon throughout my trials, illuminating the truth that my struggles, though fierce, are temporary compared to the eternal glory that awaits.

Reflecting on my path, I realize that every hardship, every moment of pain, was not just for my own growth but also to equip me to assist others navigating similar trials. The purpose of my journey has been to pass on the knowledge of God's grace and healing, providing hope to those who may feel ensnared by their circumstances.

Throughout my life, I have aspired to be the expressed image of God. I desire that when others look at me, they see Him and not the scars of my past or the pain I have endured. Through God's transformative power, I have been remade, not as a fractured vessel but as one whole and complete in Him. This message of renewal is what I aim to impart to others—that regardless of how tumultuous one's journey may be, in God there is victory and restoration.

This walk of faith is not devoid of challenges, as Apostle Paul eloquently describes in Romans 7. He talks about the internal conflict between the desire to do good and the ever-present sin that battles within. Like Paul, I have experienced this war within my members, a struggle between spirit and flesh that is common to us all. Yet, I stand today as a testament to the power of perseverance and the faithfulness of God who delivers us.

In this chapter, I want to affirm that no matter how many battles we face, victory is assured because we are supported by the host of Heaven's armies. The enemy's attempts to undermine our faith through doubt and deceit are formidable, but the identity we have in Christ equips us to overcome. We are fighting not just for survival but for the right to thrive and claim the promises God has laid before us.

I believe God sends people into our lives when we need them the most, guiding us to the next level of our journey. My conversion wasn't an easy one, as I was plagued by my past and burdened by the inability to forgive myself. I felt that the world saw me in that same unforgiving light. However, the Word of God teaches us that love covers a multitude of sins and reassures us that God casts our sins into the sea of forgetfulness. So, we have no reason to hold on to what we've repented from and turned away from.

My encounters with spiritual mentors and the prophetic words spoken over me have reinforced my mission and clarified my purpose. These divine appointments have taught me the importance of community and the power of vulnerability in fostering spiritual growth and resilience. They have shown me that healing often comes through confronting and speaking out our pain, not in isolation but in communion with those who guide and uplift us.

I don't know what I would have done without the support of my elder at that time, who was the music director for the choir. He helped teach me the foundations of worship and praise. In my darkest moments, I found solace in praising God. My worship is genuine and heartfelt. When people ask me why I worship the way I do, I tell them it's because I've realized that God is the only reason I made it through.

My sister in Christ embraced me in a loving and motherly way. She softened my heart and gave me opportunities to grow and develop without feeling judged. Although we did not have frequent conversations, First Lady took the time to share her wisdom with me, teaching me to trust in God and be obedient to Him. Her insights were instrumental in my spiritual development, and I am thankful for the moments she prayed for me and encouraged me to embrace my potential.

My Bishop constantly reminded us to seek God for ourselves, to build a strong personal relationship with Him, and to forget the past. Knowing that we are new creatures in Christ, we must walk in this new life with authority and dominion over all things as commanded by God since the beginning of time. My elder would always pray for me and encourage me to look beyond my circumstances, helping me to focus on cultivating a deeper relationship with God.

I've had moments where God sent divine connections into my life, people who prayed me through difficult times and encouraged me to press forward. These individuals, who were seasonal in my life, were crucial in my journey. The Bible tells us that Jesus left the ninety-nine sheep to find the one that went astray, and I am grateful that the Lord never gave up on me. Each time I strayed, He brought me back into His fold.

The enemy wants us to be isolated, separated from what makes us strong. Each time I distanced myself from God, He was always there, sending someone to guide me back to where I belonged. I've learned to discern the people God sends and those who are meant to walk with me temporarily. Along this journey, I've lost some good friends, but I've also found a deeper, more real relationship with God.

I wouldn't change anything about my journey because it led me to this deeper connection with God. I would never trade the trials for anything because they shaped who I am today. I don't need drugs or alcohol to fill the void anymore. I just need to be at the feet of Jesus and give Him everything because He knows my past and where I'm going. God sees me and my prayer is always that when He sees me, He sees Himself reflected in me. I am made in His image and likeness, and no one can take that from me. That's one significant lesson from my journey toward healing.

The healing journey is deeply personal, yet universally resonant. It involves forgiving those who have wronged us and releasing the burden of past hurts. It requires a conscious decision to forgive, sometimes without receiving an apology, and to trust in God's grace and mercy to heal and restore. This process is not easy, but it is necessary for true freedom and fulfillment.

As I close this chapter and this book, my message is one of hope and encouragement. Greater things are indeed coming for each of us. Our greatness arrives when we choose to break free from the chains of our past, embrace the present, and step into the future prepared for us by God. It is a future where we can truly arise and shine, for our light has come, and the glory of the Lord has risen upon us.

To everyone who has walked this path with me through the pages of this book, know that your greater is coming. It begins the moment you decide to let go and let God fully direct your life. As we look forward to a future filled with promise, remember that we are called to soar like eagles, run without growing weary, and reap the harvest if we do not give up.

A LETTER TO MY
HEALED SELF

Dear Healed Me,

Growing up was already hell, but the pit was far worse. It's an internal place that nobody can see or understand, yet you know it's there. The enemy is in the pit, whispering lies and reinforcing every trauma, ensuring you remain bound and hopeless.

In this darkness, the enemy thrives. You become numb to anything good. Every accident, every broken relationship, every disappointment, it all feeds into the lie that you're worthless. It's as if the river of life has turned into a flood, overwhelming and swallowing you whole.

But God did not leave me there. He used people around me to lift me out of that pit. It wasn't easy. The enemy wanted to keep me trapped, but God's love and promises are stronger than any lie. He began to teach me how to speak life over myself, and to declare His promises even when I couldn't see them.

I needed to understand that my worth was not determined by my past or my trauma but by who God says I am. His love is unconditional, and His grace is sufficient. I am a new creation in Christ, and the old has passed away. He has given me beauty for ashes, joy for mourning, and a garment of praise instead of a spirit of despair.

Today, I walk in the light of God's love. His Word is my weapon, and His Spirit is my guide. I have learned to forgive myself because He has forgiven me. I have learned to love myself because He loves me. I am no longer a victim but a victor.

God's plans for me are to prosper me, to give me hope and a future. He has turned my mourning into dancing, and my sorrow into joy. I serve Him with all my heart, and I trust in His promises. I am grateful for every person He has placed in my life to help me along this journey.

I no longer live in fear because perfect love casts out fear. I am no longer bound by the past because whom the Son sets free is free indeed. I am a child of God, loved and cherished, and I walk in the authority He has given me.

I encourage you, wherever you are, to trust in God's promises. No matter how dark it may seem, His light can pierce through the darkness. He can turn your sorrow into joy and give you a future filled with hope. Hold on to His Word, declare His promises, and walk in the light of His love.

With love and faith,
My Healed Self

POWERFUL DECLARATIONS

Below, you will find a collection of declarations that I have composed to address some of the most profound challenges we face in our spiritual and emotional lives. These declarations are specifically tailored to provide comfort and guidance for those grappling with anxiety, depression, and issues of identity, as well as to reaffirm the enduring promises of God.

It is my hope that these words will serve as a source of solace and inspiration, helping you to navigate through your moments of doubt and to embrace the peace and assurance that God promises to each of us.

Please scan the QR codes provided (on the following page) alongside each topic to listen to an audio recording of the declaration, enhancing your experience as you reflect and find guidance through these words.

* * *

Declarations

Declaration Over Addiction
Declaration Over Anxiety
Declaration Over Depression
Declaration Over Identity
Declaration Over God's Promises

Introduction

Declaration Over Addiction

Declaration Over Anxiety

Declaration Over Depression

Declaration Over Identity

Declaration Over Promises

ACKNOWLEDGMENTS

I want to express my deepest gratitude to everyone who contributed to making this book possible. To everyone who has supported me with your prayers and wisdom, I am deeply appreciative.

To my mom, *Claudette*, thank you for your endless love, support, and encouragement.

To my dear friends— *Capricia, Yolande, Madonna, Michelle,* and the one I call '*Friend*' —thank you for pushing me beyond my comfort zone and never letting me settle.

To my *Iron Sharpeneth Iron* — thank you for seeing me when I did not want to be seen. Thank you for speaking life into me when I was in a cocoon and, most importantly, for showing me what faith and prayer can accomplish.

To my *church family* — thank you for loving me out of the pit.

To my *mentors* — your wisdom and guidance have been invaluable.

And to my *readers* — this book exists because of you. Thank you for allowing me to share my testimony with you.

ABOUT THE AUTHOR

 Jaun Malcolm– a licensed minister, intercessor, mentor, educator, author, and photographer– was born in Jamaica, W.I., and immigrated to the United States during her early years. From a young age, Jaun found solace in the arts, garnering accolades for her talents in drawing and writing. Her life has been marked by significant challenges, including a life-altering near-death experience in 2008, which deepened her faith and defined her life's purpose.

Inspired by Isaiah 61:1, Jaun is passionate about her calling to bring good tidings to the meek, heal the brokenhearted, and proclaim liberty to captives. She shares a powerful message of hope, redemption, and salvation, touching the lives of those ready to listen. With her profound grasp of the Scriptures, Jaun acts as a dedicated conduit for God, guiding others toward spiritual growth, transformation, and the fulfillment of God's promises for all Believers.

www.ingramcontent.com/pod-product-compliance
Lightning Source LLC
Chambersburg PA
CBHW051219120626
46547CB00013B/1426